TWENTIETH CENTURY INTERPRETATIONS
OF

THE PRAISE OF FOLLY

TWENTIETH CENTURY INTERPRETATIONS
OF

THE PRAISE

OF FOLLY

A Collection of Critical Essays

Edited by
KATHLEEN WILLIAMS

Prentice-Hall, Inc. A SPECTRUM BOOK *Englewood Cliffs, N. J.*

Current printing (last number):
10 9 8 7 6 5 4 3 2 1

PRENTICE-HALL INTERNATIONAL, INC. (*London*)
PRENTICE-HALL OF AUSTRALIA, PTY. LTD. (*Sydney*)
PRENTICE-HALL OF CANADA, LTD. (*Toronto*)
PRENTICE-HALL OF INDIA PRIVATE LIMITED (*New Delhi*)
PRENTICE-HALL OF JAPAN, INC. (*Tokyo*)

Contents

1-155057

Introduction

by Kathleen Williams

The Praise of Folly was written in 1509 in Latin, the language in which the humanist Erasmus, like his close friend Sir Thomas More, habitually wrote, aiming as he did at an international audience of educated men to whom Latin was a second living language. Erasmus was a prolific author, but this brilliant and complex work has proved over the centuries to be his most popular production. Forty-three editions were published during Erasmus' lifetime, and from the sixteenth century to the present it has repeatedly been reprinted and translated into English. Its fascination is the fascination of Erasmus' mind: subtle, penetrating, imaginative. Like the *Utopia* of his friend More, it is still relevant to our own age and can still sharpen our minds, for it is concerned not with the topical only but with lasting tendencies of the human mind and condition. Of all the works of the early Renaissance of northern Europe, *The Praise of Folly* and *Utopia* have perhaps most to say to us. We can read them as we would the writings of a contemporary, without feeling that their writers are alien to us and have to be interpreted. None the less, though *The Praise of Folly* seems now as relevant to man's affairs as it did in the sixteenth century, some account of Erasmus' life and interests, and of his relation to the mental and spiritual concerns of his time, may make it easier to understand the details of the work and the particular tendencies of the age which Erasmus presents to us *sub specie aeternitatis*.

Erasmus was born in or near Rotterdam, Holland, in (probably) 1466. He was himself never certain of the year, and it may have been later. His father, Gerard, was a priest, and of his mother, who died of the plague in 1483, nothing is known except her name, Margaret. As a priest of the Catholic Church, still the one Church of the West and as yet untouched by the Reformation which made so great a stir in his son's lifetime, the father was under a vow of celibacy, but he would appear to have established a more or less lasting liaison with Margaret; at least we know that Erasmus was the second son. Many priests, doubtless, made irregular alliances of this kind, and it does not appear that Erasmus was under any particular stigma as a result of his illegitimate birth; but illegitimacy did disqualify a man from holding Church benefices, and later in his life he had to obtain a papal dis-

1

pensation so that he could accept a benefice. At about the age of four he was sent to school at Gouda, and at nine he went to the famous school of the chapter of St. Lebuin at Deventer, with a short period as a chorister at Utrecht. Erasmus was never pleased with the schooling he received, for he disliked the old-fashioned medieval methods and textbooks which still largely prevailed in the schools and universities, and in his adult life he was associated with men like John Colet, Dean of St. Paul's, who established his own school. The humanist scholars of the Renaissance were anxious that a purer, more truly classical, Latinity should replace the "barbarism" of medieval Latin, and they wished the precepts of the gospels to replace what seemed to them the niggling questions of the failing scholasticism of the Middle Ages. But Erasmus does seem to have gained something from the school at Deventer. Some of the masters belonged to the community of the Brethren of the Common Life, the so-called *Devotio Moderna,* with its devotion to the Bible and its evangelical piety of a kind the adult Erasmus was to appreciate. Some of the Brethren, moreover, were taking their own steps toward the reformation of education.

Both Erasmus' parents died while he was at Deventer, and he and his brother returned home to Gouda, where they were left in the care of guardians. Up to this point Erasmus had received an education as good as was available to him. His father appears to have been something of a scholar: he had traveled to Italy, was versed in Latin, and even knew a little Greek, a very unusual thing in his day. Erasmus was now of an age to enter a university, and in later life he was resentful that he had not been sent there. As it was, he and his brother went for another two years to school at Bois-le-Duc, a severe institution which, Erasmus believed, had no aim beyond that of fitting its pupils for entering a monastic life. Then, persuaded by his guardians and by a friend and schoolfellow who was himself a monk, Erasmus yielded and entered the monastery of Steyn, near Gouda, a community of regular Augustinian canons. Erasmus was now probably about twenty years old; his elder brother had already yielded to persuasion. Erasmus took his vows probably in 1488. He was unhappy at Steyn, lacking intellectual companionship and responding painfully to the physical austerities of monastic life. Erasmus was always of a delicate constitution, and he was fastidious. Doubtless he suffered from the—as he saw it—pointless discomfort of life at Steyn. Little is known of his years there, for few letters (Erasmus was a fine and a prolific letter-writer) have survived from this period, but he appears to have devoted himself to the writing of Latin verses and to the development of that wonderfully elegant Latin style for which he was to become famous. He always remained hostile to the monasticism he knew in practice, whatever he may have thought of it as a theoretical way of life.

In 1492 Erasmus was ordained priest, possibly in the hope of leaving the monastery, and the next year his chance came. He was appointed secretary to an important churchman, the Bishop of Cambray, who proposed to travel to Rome and would have use for a skilled Latinist like Erasmus. But the journey to Rome was canceled, and instead Erasmus gained the Bishop's permission, and his financial support, to study in the college of Montaigu at Paris, the most famous university of the day. Here he obtained the degree of doctor of theology, though he found little to please or instruct him in the sterility of the last days of scholasticism, the quibbles and quiddities of Thomists and Scotists and Ockhamists. *Magistri nostri,* as the doctors of theology liked to be called, have with the monks a place of honor in the satire of *The Praise of Folly.* But he continued his own reading—in Greek now as well as in Latin—and writing, and he was making himself into one of the most learned men, as well as the most elegant Latinist, of his time. By letter he introduced himself to a leading Parisian humanist, Robert Gaguin, and so entered the world of Renaissance humanism to which he was to contribute so much, never again to leave it. He published a book of Latin verse, and during this period at Steyn and in Paris he wrote or began to write works that were not to be published for some years; for example, the *Antibarbari,* an imaginary conversation directed, from a humanist point of view, at the old-fashioned scholastic and religious establishment. To supplement his small income, he took pupils, among them William Blount, the heir of Lord Mountjoy, with whom he established a lasting friendship.

In 1498 Erasmus visited England in Blount's company and received a great welcome from the English humanists, to whom he remained close for the rest of their lives. William Warham, Archbishop of Canterbury, became his friend and patron, and he met the young Thomas More and above all John Colet, who at that time made the greatest impression on his mind. Colet, with other humanist scholars such as Grocyn and Linacre, was open to the influence of contemporary Florentine Platonism, and had, like the Florentines themselves, blended the influence of Plato and that of the Bible. Colet and his friends had produced what H. R. Trevor-Roper calls "a new movement, Platonist and Pauline, by which Erasmus . . . was at once inspired." [1] Erasmus was now confirmed in his devotion to two related ends: evangelical piety and Greek and Latin learning. During his life of extraordinary intellectual activity, his learning and his energy were to be turned chiefly to the production of works which could contribute to the growth of what he himself called *Philosophia Christi,* the philosophy of Christ: he translated the New Testament from Greek into Latin and established a more reliable text; he translated the church fathers; he labored at the printing presses of Basel and Venice, exploiting to the full the new art of printing to bring great Christian works in as

[1] *Men and Events: Historical Essays* (New York, 1957), p. 40.

pure a form as possible into the hands of all those who could read
Latin, and making use of the classical scholarship of Italy, especially
the strict and precise textual scholarship of a great Italian humanist,
Lorenzo Valla. All this was in the service of *Philosophia Christi*; Erasmus hoped to bring about the abandonment of the now sterile intel-
lectuality of the schoolmen and of the mechanical apparatus of indulgences, pilgrimages, and saint-worship, which had replaced, he felt,
the true and living faith of the gospels and the early church. For a
while he seemed to have succeeded. His influence spread widely over
Europe during his lifetime, until the Reformation broke upon the
north and the lines of Protestant and Catholic were drawn; thereupon
conditions became too harsh for the gentle and moderate *Philosophia
Christi*.

To return to Erasmus' first visit to England, it was there in the
congenial company of his humanist friends that he pursued his study
of Greek, refusing a permanent place in Oxford as he was to refuse
all advancement which could have encroached upon his freedom. He
had, he said himself, "an immoderate love of liberty." After his return
to France he published *Adagia*, a collection of sayings which first made
his reputation throughout Europe, and in 1504 a work of piety, the
Enchiridion Militis Christiani, the manual of the Christian soldier.
In 1505 he was in England, and in 1506 in Italy. From 1509 to 1514
he was again in England, except for a brief visit to France. In England
he made new friends and improved his relationships with old ones, including More, at whose house he spent much of his time, though he
also lectured on Greek at Cambridge. It was in 1509, on his journey
from Italy to England, that, according to his own account, he had the
idea of writing *The Praise of Folly*, which he wrote in More's house
as he waited for his books to come. The Greek word *Moria* (Folly) re-
minded him, he tells us in the dedication of the work, of the name of
his friend More, and it struck him that though More's name was so
like that of Folly, yet the man himself was very far removed from it.
And indeed in this paradoxical pun there is contained the shaping
idea of *The Praise of Folly*. Just as Thomas More, later to be sainted
by his Church, was a man of *festivitas*, of wit and gaiety of manner,
but of deep seriousness, so is Erasmus' *Moriae Encomium* a work
which combines lightness of manner with a seriousness of content
which reaches to some of the profoundest paradoxes of Christianity.
The work was written, according to Erasmus, in only a few days, and
one can understand that once the idea had come to him it would
release the fund of classical knowledge that he now had at his finger-
tips, and would release too his moral convictions, his hatred of war
and cruelty, of pomposity and pride of place, of the pretensions of
magistri nostri, of theologians and monks and friars, plagiarist writers
and grammarians. On its appearance *The Praise of Folly* was received

with delight, but also with resentment at least on the part of those who felt that they had been satirized.

From England, in 1514, Erasmus went to Basel, where his translation of the New Testament was printed. He paid short visits thereafter to his friends in England, but he did not live in England again. He received a great welcome from the humanist scholars of Germany, and during the following years he saw through the press his New Testament (an improved Greek text with notes, and a Latin translation) and his edition of Jerome, working closely with the great printer Froben. From the time of these "daring theological works," to quote from his biographer Huizinga, Erasmus "made himself the centre of the scientific study of divinity, as he was at the same time the centre and touchstone of classic erudition and literary taste. His authority constantly increased in all countries, his correspondence was prodigiously augmented." [2] In 1516 he was given the honorific title of councillor to the young Charles V; the position carried a pension and resulted in the writing of a moral treatise on the education of princes, *Institutio Principis Christiani*. With a prebend in Courtray and a benefice in England, Erasmus was now more comfortable financially. But his wandering life of learning continued. From 1517 he lived in the university city of Louvain, and in 1518 visited the printing house at Basel to work there at editions of his writings.

It was in these years that the Reformation began with the polemics of Martin Luther; and the extremism of Luther in the cause of reform, and the answering extremism of the church authorities, created an atmosphere in which Erasmus' more temperate efforts to draw the church back to a practical piety could no longer continue to be effective. Erasmus was opposed to any persecution of Luther; both Luther and his enemies expected support from him, but he was reluctant to give it to either. He wanted reform only within the church: reform of the monasteries, abolition of the mechanical paraphernalia of indulgences which Luther also hated, and an end to the superstitious veneration of relics and similar abuses. But with Luther's theological innovations he had no sympathy, and he saw that in the situation which now prevailed there was no hope of the peaceful purifying of the faith, of the return to the gospels that he had hoped to bring about by his writings and perhaps above all by his translations, which brought the Bible and the church fathers in purer form to a reading public greatly increased by the new art of printing. Erasmus himself in the new polemical atmosphere became suspect: it was said that he had laid the egg that Luther hatched. Soon after his death, *The Praise of Folly* was prohibited by the ecclesiastical authorities in Franche-Comté, and in the following years his works were prohibited in various Catholic countries.

[2] *Erasmus of Rotterdam* (New York, 1952), p. 91.

Erasmus has often been criticized for his refusal to commit himself wholly to either side in the Reformation struggle. Perhaps he was reluctant to face theological controversy, but no doubt he also hoped, as long as hope was possible, to use his authority and influence to mediate between the two positions. But most of all, Erasmus was not a man to believe in simple and extreme answers to problems. *The Praise of Folly* shows us the bent of his mind. He sees all sides of a question, and folly as he presents it is neither wholly good nor wholly bad. Rather, it is an inescapable part of our nature, and though it brings about some sad and regrettable things, it also produces things we could not live without. *The Praise of Folly* goes further still in double-sidedness: who, in the end, can be sure of always being able to distinguish folly, in some of its aspects, from wisdom itself? May not worldly wisdom be called folly, and is not the truly Christian life folly when regarded from the point of view of such wisdom? The height of the Christian life, its completest wisdom, is the foolishness of the cross. For a man so open to the ambiguity of life, it would be natural to see some wisdom and some folly in both the reformers and their opponents. One aspect of the foolishness of both sides was their indifference, even, Erasmus thought, in some cases their hostility, to his beloved *bonae literae*—i.e., literature. It was through good writing, with all that that implies of purity and elegance and precision, of wisdom and moderation, that Erasmus had hoped to reform the morals and the faith of the time. But he felt more and more that this aim was threatened on all sides. He wrote to a friend in March 1519: "I know quite certainly that the barbarians on all sides have conspired to leave no stone unturned till they have suppressed *bonae literae*." And again, "This is the source and hot-bed of all this tragedy; incurable hatred of linguistic study and the *bonae literae*." [3]

In 1521 Erasmus left Louvain, a theologically conservative city where perhaps he felt himself under too much pressure to join the fight against Luther, and went to Basel, where he lived until 1529. At Basel, though he suffered increasingly from the internal disorder which always troubled him, he toiled more vigorously than ever at his life's work, that of making available the sources of Christianity in as pure a form as he could. New works, and new editions of his existing works, flowed from the printing press, and here too he brought out in final form the *Colloquies*, by virtue of which, together with *The Praise of Folly*, he is still alive to us. Witty, rich, lively, and often satiric, the *Colloquies* became popular immediately and remained so for two hundred years.

In 1524 Erasmus was at last, pressed as he was by prominent and powerful men including King Henry VIII, reluctantly persuaded to write against Luther. When he did so, he challenged Luther not on

[3] Quoted by Huizinga, *op. cit.,* pp. 137–38.

any superficial subject of ceremony or ritual, but at the heart of his doctrine. He wrote on free will, *De libero arbitrio,* which drew from Luther in his turn an extreme statement of his position, *De servo arbitrio.* In these last years Erasmus, who always claimed to long for peace, was caught up in controversy with others as well as Luther. It is typical of that balanced mind, disliking all extremes, which made him seem changeable and Protean to those less flexible than himself, that he even attacked certain tendencies of that classical humanism he had done so much to build. His aim had been always to reconcile classical learning and the love of Christ; he objected to *bonae literae* which savored more of paganism than of Christianity, and he objected to a slavish and pedantic following of the style and the very words of such writers as Cicero. These things he attacked in the mocking *Ciceronianus,* which brought him new enemies.

Meanwhile Protestantism and controversy spread in Basel, and with both sides as usual anxious to make use of the authority of his scholarship and the brilliance of his pen Erasmus felt that it was time to go if his independence was to be preserved. He moved to Freiburg im Breisgau, and there he still worked, on *Ecclesiastes,* a work on the art of preaching, an activity which he always regarded as important. This was to have been dedicated to his friend Bishop John Fisher, but Fisher like Thomas More was beheaded in 1535. Not every humanist scholar, however willing to avoid extremes, was able to escape as Erasmus had done the violence of the age. But Erasmus himself was soon to die. He returned to Basel in the summer of 1535 to see a new printing of the *Adagia* and other work through the press. Here, busy to the end, he fell ill and died among his friends in 1536. His last words, in Latin and in his native Low German, called upon God and upon Christ.

The Praise of Folly can be seen to be an integral part of Erasmus' life. It is a brilliant satire, but like all satire it implies, through its attacks, what its writer holds to and loves. Good writing and good living, both enlivened by the love of Christ and by a simple faith, are implied everywhere as values, through the dazzling complications of Folly's speech. Martin Dorp's earnest advice to stifle objections to *The Praise of Folly* by writing a praise of wisdom, which would make all well, rightly exasperated Erasmus, for *The Praise of Folly* is also a praise of wisdom. The work was quickly written, but by the time he wrote it Erasmus had a great store of learning and of well-seasoned thoughts ready in his mind to pour out when the idea came to him of writing an encomium of Folly, put into the mouth of Folly herself. The idea has the great merit of an almost infinite flexibility. Almost any form of conduct is foolish to someone else, and so folly can be now the pomposity of the learned or their ineffectuality in everyday life, now the innocence of children, now the coldness of the Stoic, the

warmth of the loving, and even the unworldliness of the saint. Erasmus'
mouthpiece, Folly, embraces them all.

The Praise of Folly is technically an encomium, a eulogy, a form
which in classical rhetoric had its own guiding rules (listed, in the
present volume, in the essay by Hoyt H. Hudson).[4] Along with the
tradition of serious eulogy, there had grown up even as early as
classical times a tradition of *mock* eulogy. Erasmus refers to this tradition in his dedication of his work to Thomas More. He points out
that, trifle though the mock encomium is, important writers had not
been ashamed to use it, and he lists several examples, including
Lucian's praises of a fly and a parasite. The name of Lucian suggests
the opportunities for satiric comment which the mock encomium
naturally offers, just as the mock heroic, also present in at least
rudimentary and sporadic form in the classical period, offered satiric
opportunities which Dryden, Pope, and Swift were later to exploit.
Both Erasmus and More were great admirers of that accomplished
ironist and satirist, Lucian, and had translated some of his works; but
for most of their contemporaries Lucian was a destructive satirist,
a sneerer who attacked everything. Erasmus is careful to suggest in
the dedicatory epistle that, whatever people may think of Lucian, he
himself is not writing a merely destructive general attack. He hints
that the *Praise* treats of apparently frivolous topics in a manner profoundly suggestive: "I think that I have praised folly in a way not
altogether foolish." Thus, as in his relating of Folly's Greek name,
Moria, to the name of his witty and wise friend (whose *Utopia,* written
a few years later, is likewise a foolish fancy with wisdom at the heart
of it), Erasmus points again and again to the serious meaning of his
joking eulogy. The mock encomium—again like mock epic—readily
lends itself to irony, and another way of defining *The Praise of Folly*
is to classify it, as some of the writers in this volume have done, as
part of the vast Renaissance literature of paradox; again, the second
but first-written book of *Utopia,* taken alone, could be seen as a
paradox, a Praise of Nowhere. This literature took many forms, and
indeed many very different writers learned from the influential *Praise
of Folly,* but essentially the literature of paradox is shaped to express
ambiguity, to stress the coexistence of apparently irreconcilable truths.
Such a way of seeing and expressing things went back to that quintes-
sential ironist Socrates, as the men of the Renaissance were well aware.
Erasmus carefully reminds us of Socrates in Folly's reference to a
passage very familiar to the learned of his day, from Plato's *Symposium.*
In it Alcibiades compares Socrates to the figures of Silenus; "the Sileni
of Alcibiades," Erasmus calls them, statuettes of the satyr-like friend
of Dionysus which when opened were found to contain images of the

[4] See pp. 21–39.

gods. The point of the comparison was to praise Socrates' ability to see through the outside of things, however unpromising they may appear, to their inner meaning. The reference to the *Symposium* draws our attention to the doubleness of things; the passage in Folly's speech runs:

> For first of all, the fact is that all human affairs, like the Sileni of Alcibiades, have two aspects, each quite different from the other; even to the point that what at first blush (as the phrase goes) seems to be death may prove, if you look further into it, to be life. What at first sight is beautiful may really be ugly; the apparently wealthy may be poorest of all; the disgraceful, glorious; the learned, ignorant; . . . In brief, you find all things suddenly reversed, when you open up the Silenus.[5]

Even this passage tends to simplify the actual practice of *The Praise of Folly*. Erasmus' idea of putting the mock praise of folly into the mouth of Folly herself adds another dimension to the ironies implicit in the paradoxical mock encomium, and one soon finds that it is not enough simply to invert Folly's statements to get at the truth, for the fact that Folly is speaking sets up a position analogous, as Walter Kaiser has pointed out, to that which prevails in one of the ancient stock paradoxes, that of the Cretan who says all Cretans are liars.[6] This is an impenetrable paradox which cannot be resolved into simple positive or negative statements, and neither can the utterances of Folly. In Erasmus' extended paradox we are presented not with a choice between true or false statements but with a view of the complexities of truth, truth which may be also false, if looked at from another point of view, and falsity which may also be true. The final truth of *The Praise of Folly* lies not in particular passages but in the work as a whole, as a statement about the complexities of life.

And more than a statement, for by allowing Folly to sound her own praises Erasmus is able to show us folly, in all its multifarious meanings, actually articulating itself. We are not simply told that this or that is foolish (and often, at the same time, wise; for how is it always possible to distinguish accurately between foolishness and wisdom?); we listen to foolishness displaying itself. So years later did Jonathan Swift, writing in the tradition of Erasmus, display to us the madness of the world, and by implication that which is sane in it, through the writing of a muddleheaded fool, the pretended author of *A Tale of a Tub* (the phrase itself occurs in John Wilson's 1668 translation of *The Praise of Folly*, in a reference to the absurd names that writers give themselves and their books). In *The Praise of Folly* as in the Erasmian *Tale of a Tub* we do not merely agree with the picture of human foolishness and the moral evaluations which that picture

---

[5] *The Praise of Folly*, tr. Hoyt H. Hudson (Princeton, 1941), p. 36.
[6] See p. 79.

implies; rather, we live imaginatively through a moral experience which stirs us to fresh insights. Other works—for example Brandt's *The Ship of Fools*—had been *about* fools and folly, but only Erasmus invented a method by which folly could display itself before us in all its human complication. The philosophers say that to live a life of folly, ignorance, and error is to be unhappy. No indeed, says Folly; this is to be human. "For what that passes among mortals everywhere is not full of folly, done by fools in the presence of fools?" [7] None of us can escape some kind of folly. Love is folly from the point of view of the strict neo-stoic moralist, to whom virtue is reason, and passion vice; yet what is more foolish than the cold, rigid, friendless existence of the wholly reasonable man, whom life passes by? Again, has any solemn philosopher had so great an effect on the life and actions of men as have the writers of foolish fables, of fictions like those of Themistocles or Numa or Menenius Agrippa? Thus the fictional form in which Erasmus himself is writing is foolishness—for Erasmus often in this way includes his own activities as part of the human folly which Folly praises. As a human being, the satirist himself is caught in the inescapable folly of mankind. From one point of view the virtues themselves are foolish, and that holiness which, unutterable joy though it is, is only the slightest taste of the happiness hereafter.

Thus paradox after paradox unfolds within the governing paradox of Folly's praise of folly. There is much particular satire on war, on warlike and worldly popes, on friars, on monks, on scholastic philosophy; and it is this to which exception was taken in Erasmus' lifetime. But still more important is the vision of which the particular satire is only a part: the vision of man caught by his very nature in folly, but a folly capable of reaching the heights of self-sacrifice and sanctity as well as playing benevolently about the small daily concerns of life. Erasmus' work is one of the greatest and profoundest examinations of the paradox of the wise fool, which was one of the familiar ideas of the late Middle Ages and the Renaissance and which we know best from the fools of Shakespeare. Folly herself reminds us of the Greek proverb "Even a foolish man will often speak a word in season." [8] Erasmus is, as Walter Kaiser and other scholars have pointed out, "one of the seminal minds of the modern world." [9] Rabelais, Montaigne, Shakespeare, Jonson, Ariosto, Cervantes, Swift, all owe much to that penetrating and wide-ranging mind with its capacity to hold many ideas in solution and to see, in one inclusive vision, the capacity for warmth and frigidity, for joy and sorrow, for good and evil, for self-sacrifice and self-indulgence, in the life of the wise fool, man.

Erasmus is one of our great ironists, for only irony with its capacity

---

[7] Hudson, *op. cit.*, p. 33.

[8] *Ibid.*, p. 125.

[9] Walter R. Kaiser, *Praisers of Folly* (Cambridge, Mass., 1963), p. 91.

to mean two or more conflicting things at one and the same moment, can do justice to the vision he brought to bear on human life. He meant much and taught much to the great successors I have mentioned, but we must not forget that Professor Kaiser's phrase is "one of the seminal minds of the *modern* world." Erasmus' influence has extended through other great writers to our own time, and we can respond to him in an age when once more truth seems to be many-faceted, when civilization seems poised between a past outgrown and a future only partly visible to us. If it is true that irony belongs to such periods of transition, of which Erasmus' age, poised between the Middle Ages and the developing Renaissance, was one, then we can surely enjoy his irony, for we too strive to reconcile two worlds, one passing and the other coming obscurely into being. The wise inclusiveness, the delicate balance, of Erasmus' remarkable mind has much to teach us as we struggle to see conflicting truths as parts of one great truth, wider and more all-embracing than either.

PART ONE

Interpretations

The Praise of Folly

by Preserved Smith

The most widely read, though not the most important, work of Erasmus, the one which gave him an immediate international reputation, was *The Praise of Folly,* written just after his return from Italy, while he was waiting in More's house for the arrival of his books and was suffering from an attack of lumbago.[1]

Something of the spirit and intention of the *Folly* is revealed in the dedicatory epistle to More:

> On returning from Italy . . . I chose to amuse myself with the *Praise of Folly (Moria).* What Pallas, you will say, put that into your head? Well, the first thing that struck me was your surname More, which is just as near the name of Moria or Folly as you are far from the thing itself, from which, by general vote you are remote indeed. In the next place I surmised that this playful production of our genius would find special favor with you, disposed as you are to take pleasure in a jest of this kind, that is neither, unless I mistake, unlearned nor altogether inept. . . . For, as nothing is more trifling than to treat serious questions frivolously, so nothing is more amusing than to treat trifles in such a way as to show yourself anything but a trifler.

This last sentence gives the key to the *Folly.* It is a witty sermon, an earnest satire, a joke with an ethical purpose. Satire of this peculiar flavor, mockery with a moral, was characteristic of the age. How much of it there is in Luther, how much in Hutten, how much in Rabelais, how much in the *Epistles of Obscure Men!* Erasmus probably had many of the earlier satirists in mind, though he mentions as literary sources only classical models, beginning with the *Batrachomyomachia.*

"The Praise of Folly." *From* Erasmus, A Study of His Life, Ideals, and Place in History *by Preserved Smith (New York: Harper & Row, Publishers, Incorporated, 1923), pp. 117–28. Reprinted by permission of the publisher.*

[1] Allen, epp. 337; 222; Nichols, epp. 317 (ii, p. 5), 212. The *Encomium Moriæ* is printed LB. iv, 381 ff; also see *Stultitiæ Laus Des. Erasmi Rot. Recognovit et adnotavit* I. B. Kan. 1898. Many editions of the English versions; see *The Praise of Folly,* written by Erasmus 1509, translated by J. Wilson, 1668, ed. by Mrs. P. S. Allen, 1913.

He speaks particularly of Lucian, the author of dialogues on the fly, on the parasite, and on the ass, and of course Erasmus's careful study and translation of this author contributed to his own mastery of the ironic style. But there were certainly works nearer his own time which also influenced him. If he would have scorned the barbarous Goliardic songs, which contain a vast amount of mockery directed against the Church, he would have felt much less repulsion for the works of Poggio and Aretino, both of whom wrote *Facetiæ* with many a shrewd blow directed at superstition and human foibles. He knew them both, as well as Skelton, the English wit.

At Rome he must have become acquainted with one of the famous vehicles of caricature and lampoon, the statue of Pasquin, from which the word "pasquinade" is derived. In 1501 there had been dug up there a statue lacking nose, arms, and part of the legs, which was then believed to be a Hercules, but is now known to represent Menelaus carrying the body of Patroclus. This statue was set up by its discoverer, Cardinal Oliver Caraffa, in the Piazza Navona, near a shrine to which a procession was annually made on the day of St. Mark the Evangelist (April 25th). The gaiety of the Roman populace, seeing something absurd in the mutilated statue, began on these holidays to dress it up in a travesty of some antique deity or hero. Thus, in 1509, when Erasmus may well have been present, the fragment was decked out to represent Janus, in allusion to the war that had broken out with Venice. The immense publicity given to the statue gradually led to its being used as a convenient billboard for posting lampoons—for the people, deprived of power, sought revenge on their masters by heaping them with ridicule, thus tempering despotism with epigram. Finally the statue was named Pasquin after a citizen particularly noted for his biting tongue. By the year 1509 three thousand of these epigrams were known, and a collection of them had been published.[2]

But if Erasmus borrowed something from Pasquin, he found a more direct suggestion for his literary form in the *Narrenschiff* of Sebastian Brant, first published in 1494, and translated into Latin as *Stultifera Navis* by Locher Philomusus in 1497, and again by Erasmus's friend, Josse Bade the printer, in 1505, as *Navis Stultifera*. It appeared in the French translation of Pierre Rivière in 1497 as *La Nef des Folz du Monde*. Two English versions, one by Henry Watson, and a more famous one by Alexander Barclay, were printed under the title *Ship of Fools*, both in 1509.[3]

But every reader of the *Folly* must be struck by the amount in it

[2] See *Encyclopædia Britannica, s. v. "Pasquinade,"* and E. Rodocanachi: *Rome au temps de Jules II et de Léon X,* 1912, pp. 153 ff.

[3] Herford: *Literary Relations of England and Germany in the Sixteenth Century,* 1886, p. 324. Mrs. P. S. Allen, *op. cit.,* pp. iv f. Later Erasmus knew Brant personally, and wrote an epigram to him, LB. i, 1223.

taken from the writer's own observation. When he speaks of what is rotten in Church or state, his reflections are usually suggested by something he himself has seen. When he satirizes the pope, it is Julius II he has in mind; when he points out the asininity of the theologians, his examples are drawn from the lucubrations of his fellow student, John Major.[4] And if he drew few facts from predecessors, preferring to paint from the life, he had even less in common with their spirit. With Pasquin satire was a dagger, with Brant a scourge; with Erasmus it was a mirror. It is true that all satire starts with the axiom that the world is full of fools; but whereas some men, like Brant and Swift, take this to heart and with *sæva indignatio* gird at folly as wickedness, and at wickedness as folly, others, like Erasmus and Rabelais, find the idea infinitely amusing. So the Folly personified by the Dutch wit was neither vice nor stupidity, but a quite charming naïveté, the natural impulse of the child or of the unsophisticated man. Though her birth is derived from Pluto, she is no grim demon, but an amiable gossip, rather beneficent than malignant.

Without her, society would tumble about our ears, and the race die out—for what calculating wise man or woman would take the risk of marrying and bringing up children! Indeed, would women or children have any attraction without her?—like Sir Thomas Brown, Erasmus evidently thinks that the act of procreation is one that no wise man would willingly perform. Without Folly, says our author, there would be more care than pleasure; without her there would be no family, for marriages would be few and divorces many. Nay, there would be neither society nor government at all. Did not the wisest legislators, Numa and Minos, recognize the necessity of fooling the people? Socrates showed his good sense in declaring that a philosopher would keep away from politics; Plato was mistaken in thinking that philosophers should be kings and kings philosophers, for history has shown no states more miserable than those ruled by such.

Even the most esteemed arts own much to Folly, for medicine is mainly quackery and most lawyers are but pettifoggers. In fact, men would be far better off if they lived in a state of nature; just as, among animals, bees, that live according to their instincts, fare best, and horses, forced to unnatural labor, fare worst. So the wisest men are the most wretched, and fools and idiots, "unfrighted by bugbear tales of another world," are happiest. How much pleasure comes from hobbies, which are mere foolishness! One man delights in hunting, another in building, a third in gaming, but a sage despises all such frivolity.

Next, the follies of superstition are satirized, at first in words that remind the reader strongly of the *Enchiridion.* The analogy between the worship of the saints and the ancient polytheism is pointed out:

[4] *Cf. supra,* p. 23.

Polyphemus has become Christopher to keep his devotees safe; St. Erasmus gives them wealth; St. George is but the Christian Hercules. "But what shall I say of those who flatter themselves with the cheat of pardons and indulgences?" These fools think they can buy not only all the blessings and pleasures of this life, but heaven hereafter, and the priests encourage them in their error for the sake of filthy lucre.

Each nation, too, has its own pet foibles. England boasts the handsomest women; the Scots all claim gentle blood; the French pique themselves on good breeding and skill in polemic divinity; the Italians point to their own learning and eloquence.

Neither do the wise escape having their own peculiar follies. No race of men is more miserable than students of literature.

> When anyone had found out who was the mother of Anchises, or has lighted on some old, unusual word, such as bubsequus, bovinator, manticulator, or other like obsolete, cramped terms, or can, after a great deal of poring, spell out the inscription on some battered monument, Lord! what joy, what triumph, what congratulations upon his success, as if he had conquered Africa or taken Babylon the Great!

As for the scientists or "natural philosophers,"

> How sweetly they rave when they build themselves innumerable worlds, when they measure the sun, moon, stars, and spheres as though with a tape to an inch, when they explain the cause of thunder, the winds, eclipses, and other inexplicable phenomena, never hesitating, as though they were the private secretaries of creative Nature or had descended from the council of the gods to us, while in the meantime Nature magnificently laughs at them and at their conjectures.

In this disparaging estimate of natural science, though the speaker is Folly, we doubtless have the real opinion of Erasmus, who, in this, but followed Socrates and the ancient world in general. The theology of the divines is still more ridiculous:

> They will explain the precise manner in which original sin is derived from our first parents; they will satisfy you in what manner, by what degrees and in how long a time our Saviour was conceived in the Virgin's womb, and demonstrate how in the consecrated wafer the accidents can exist without the substance. Nay, these are accounted trivial, easy questions; they have greater difficulties behind, which, nevertheless, they solve with as much expedition as the former—namely, whether supernatural generation requires any instant of time? whether Christ, as a son, bears a double, specially distinct relation to God the Father and his Virgin Mother? whether it would be possible for the first person of the Trinity to hate the second? whether God, who took our nature upon him in the form of a man, could as well have become a woman, a devil, an ass, a gourd, or a stone?

So Folly enumerates the stupidities and injustices done by the monks, who insist that ignorance is the first essential, by kings and courtiers, by pope and cardinals whose lives contrast so painfully with their professions.

> I was lately [she continues] at a theological discussion, for I often go to such meetings, when some one asked what authority there was in the Bible for burning heretics instead of convincing them by argument? A certain hard old man, a theologian by the very look of him, not without a great deal of disdain, answered that it was the express injunction of St. Paul, when he said: "Hæreticum hominem post unam et alteram correptionem devita." [5] When he yelled these words over and over again and some were wondering what had struck the man, he finally explained that Paul meant that the heretic must be put out of life—de vita. Some burst out laughing, but others seemed to think this interpretation perfectly theological.

If the passages just quoted represent rather the lighter side of the satire, by which it was affiliated with Pasquin and the Obscure Men, there are not wanting admonitions keyed in a higher mood. If the author was a wit, he was also a scholar; if he was a man of the world, he was also a moralist; and it is less the gauds of the outer habit of fun than the solid gold of serious precept within that make *The Praise of Folly* a criticism of life with permanent literary value. If he decks his orator like Columbine to attract the crowd, he endows her with eloquence worthy of a missionary to convert them. When her cymbals have drawn an audience she forgets her part, and Folly speaks like wisdom; indeed, the most natural words to describe her animadversions are the words of Scripture: "Whom she loveth she chasteneth." Harken to her and hear the same message as that set forth by the Christian Knight, and by St. Peter himself: "To live well is the way to die well; you will best get rid of your sins by adding to your alms hatred of vice, tears of repentance, watching, prayer, and fasting, and a better life." Away with your outward ceremonies and futile works by which, as by a kind of religious mathematics, you would cheat God and the devil; learn to do right and thus to cultivate a pure and undefiled Christianity! The world then was hungry for the words of reform and of the gospel; and it was just because the satirist weighted his shafts of ridicule that they carried far, even as one can throw a heavy stone farther than the lightest feather.

Though Erasmus completed the work in the summer of 1509, and showed it in manuscript to several approving friends, he did not print it until two years later.[6] His statement that Richard Croke,[7] one of

---

[5] *I.e.,* "A man that is an heretic after the first and second admonition reject," Titus iii, 10. This incident was not invented by Erasmus, but was told him as a real occurrence by Colet. See the note in his New Testament to the verse cited.

[6] On the several editions, *Bibliotheca Belgica, Erasmus, Moria (Distribution de 2 décembre,* 1908 ff); Allen, i, p. 459; Nichols, ii, 1 ff; Mrs. P. S. Allen, *op. cit.,* introduction.

[7] See J. T. Sheppard: *Richard Croke,* 1919. Croke (c. 1489–1558) taught Greek at

his English pupils, was responsible for the publication, is either a polite fiction or else a proof that he gave it to some one else to have printed, in order to disavow it afterward, if necessary. At any rate, Erasmus went to Paris, in the spring of 1511, to see it through the press. A glimpse of his sojourn there is given in a letter,[8] written sixteen years later, by Stephen Gardiner, the statesman and prelate, at this time a servant of the humanist, and one especially skilled in dressing salads. The first edition, with a dedicatory epistle to More, dated June 9th,[9] was printed, without date, by Gilles de Gourmont at Paris in 1511. It was reprinted at Strassburg in August, 1511, and October, 1512; at Antwerp in January, 1512, and by Badius at Paris, revised by the author, in July, 1512. In all, forty editions were called for during the author's lifetime.

A commentary by Gerard Lystrius was added to the Froben edition of 1515, and to most of the subsequent reprints. It was long suspected that these notes were by Erasmus himself, and it was thought the name was but a disguise. Lystrius, however, was a real person, and the secret of his operations has only just been discovered. Erasmus, indeed, began the job himself, but later turned it over to Lystrius, a youth eager for glory. Even afterward, however, Erasmus probably furnished the bulk of the material, including a dedicatory epistle purporting to come from Lystrius and highly praising the work. As one sees by the example of Sir Walter Scott, who in anonymous reviews compared the Waverley Novels to Shakespeare's plays, this questionable practice of self-laudation in disguise was indulged in by others than by the author of the *Folly*. Lystrius, having scored an easy success with his annotations on the *Folly*, wished to collaborate further in a similar edition of the *Enchiridion*, but Erasmus refused.[10]

In 1515 Hans Holbein the younger and other artists added as marginal drawings illustrations that have often been reproduced, of which more will be said in another place.[11]

A French translation was made by George Halwyn[12] in 1517, first printed—if this is indeed the same version and not another—at Paris in 1520. New translations were made in 1642, 1670, 1713, 1780, 1789, 1826, 1867, 1870–72, and 1877. The first of several Italian versions was published in 1539; the first of many Dutch in 1560. Sir Thomas Cha-

---

Louvain, Cologne, Leipzig, and Cambridge, and filled several diplomatic missions. Erasmus probably knew him at King's College, Cambridge, where he was admitted as a scholar on April 4, 1506.

[8] Enthoven, ep. 49; Nichols, ii, p. 12.

[9] Allen, ep. 222.

[10] On Lystrius, *Bibliotheca Belgica, Erasmus, Encomium Moriæ*, ed. of 1676; Allen, ii, p. 407, Erasmus to Bucer, March 2, 1532.

[11] *Infra*, p. 152 f.

[12] Allen, ep. 641. *Cf.* ep. 660.

loner, poet and statesman, put the book into English in 1549; J. Wilson in 1668; and White Kennett, later Bishop of Peterborough, in 1683, while still an Oxford undergraduate. All these versions were frequently reprinted, and a new one added by James Copner in 1878. Folly began to speak German in 1520, Swedish in 1738, Danish in 1745,[13] Russian in 1840, Spanish in 1842, Modern Greek in 1864, Czech in 1864, and Polish in 1875.

The Praise of Folly won an immediate and striking success. Its publication marked the real beginning of that immense international reputation that put its author on a pinnacle in the world of letters hardly surpassed or even approached by anyone later save Voltaire. The editions were not small; within one month after the publication of a new reprint in March, 1515, seventeen hundred were sold,[14] and by 1522 more than twenty thousand copies had been issued in all.[15] Everyone knew, most praised, and some imitated the precious satire. James Wimpheling, a good type of the serious German humanist, later distinguished as an opponent of Luther, expressed enthusiastic admiration for it.[16] Ulrich von Hutten, in the second series of the *Epistolæ Obscurorum Virorum* (1517), warmly claimed Erasmus as the inspirer of his work.[17]

Rabelais owed much to him.[18] So did some English jest-books, especially the *Tales and Quicke Answeres,* printed about 1535, and reprinted, enlarged, as *Mery Tales, Wittie Questions, and Quicke Answeres,* in 1567.[19]

But against the general chorus of laughter and of praise, the voice of the theologians, or of some of them, made itself heard in more or less angry protest. The intensely conservative coterie at Louvain, in especial, murmured against him who had mocked their foibles. One Martin Dorp, having found that Folly's cap fitted him when he tried it on, complained directly to the author, and was answered by him and by Thomas More. The latter made the point that only enemies of good literature hated the *Moria,*[20] while Erasmus protested that his one object was to improve mankind, which he thought could be done without wounding them. He added that many of the sentiments ex-

---

[13] There is extant a MS. Icelandic translation of the *Moria* made in 1730. *Cf. An Icelandic Satire (Lof Lyginnar) by Porleifur Halldorsson,* ed. H. Hermannsson, 1915, introduction.

[14] Allen, ep. 328. April 17, 1515.

[15] LB. ix, 360.

[16] Allen, ep. 224.

[17] *Epistolæ Obscurorum Virorum,* ed. Stokes, 1910, p. 235, and other references, for which see index. Allen, ep. 363.

[18] Thuasne: *Études sur Rabelais,* 1906, chap. ii.

[19] H. de Vocht: *De Invloed van Erasmus op de Engelsche Tooneelliteratuur der XVIe en XVIIe Eeuven,* 1908.

[20] More to Dorp, Bruges, October 21, 1515, LB. App. ep. 513; *Mori Opera,* 1689, pp. 284–300.

pressed by Folly were the direct opposite of his own; and that he did not see why theologians should be so sensitive as a class, whereas kings, navigators, and physicians were equally held up to ridicule.[21]

Renewed and incessant attacks kept Erasmus busy defending himself throughout life. He protested that he had twitted no one by name but himself,[22] apparently agreeing with Mrs. Gamp, "which, no names being mentioned, no offence can be took"—and he added that Leo X, having read the book through, only laughed, and said, "I am glad our Erasmus is in the *Moria*." [23]

Among the few adverse judgments expressed by humanists, that of Stephen Dolet, "the martyr of the Renaissance," is notable:

> Most persons praise the *Encomium Moriæ*, many really admire it; yet, if you examine it, the impudence of Erasmus will strike you rather than the real force of his language. He laughs, jokes, makes fun, irritates, inveighs, and raises a smile even at Christ himself.[24]

Some of the Protestant Reformers, like Œcolampadius, loved the *Moria*,[25] whereas others, like Luther, were repelled by it. Luther quotes from it, though not by name and without expressing any opinion of it, in his lectures on the Psalms, late in the year 1516.[26] One might think that he would have relished the attack on the old Church, as a help to his own cause, but he was soon heard to cry out against such an ally. In his own copy (Basle, 1532) he wrote:[27]

> When Erasmus wrote his *Folly*, he begot a daughter like himself. He turns, twists, and bites like an awl, but he, as a fool, has written true folly.

Another satire, of far less importance, which, though published anonymously, brought some trouble on its author, was a tiny dialogue entitled *Julius excluded from Heaven*,[28] which represented the pope as vainly seeking admission to paradise. Apparently written not long after the death of Julius II (February 21, 1513), it was first published in 1517, and was at once attributed to Erasmus by Scheurl, by Pirckheimer, and by Luther, as well as by other friends who were in the secret of the authorship. He endeavored, by elaborate equivocation, amounting almost but not quite to denial, to mislead prelates and

---

[21] Allen, ep. 337; cf. epp. 304, 347.

[22] Allen, ep. 739; cf. LB. iv, 487A.

[23] Allen, ep. 749. Cf. the *Adage*, "offas ostendere," LB. ii, 461.

[24] R. C. Christie: *Étienne Dolet*, 1899, p. 191.

[25] Allen, ep. 224.

[26] *Luthers Werke*, Weimar, iv, 442, cf. *Nachträge*, p. viii.

[27] *Luther's Briefwechsel*, ed. Enders, ix, 254.

[28] Reprinted in Böcking: *Hutteni Opera*, 1859–66, iv, 421, and in Jortin's *Life of Erasmus*, 1758–60, ii, 600–622. Translated in Froude's *Life and Letters of Erasmus*. Pastor, *History of the Popes*, English, vi, 438 n., wrongly attributes it to Faustus Andrelinus. Jortin, *loc. cit.*, Nichols, ii, p. 446, and Allen, ep. 502, introduction, prove it to be by Erasmus.

others inclined to take offence at the bold mockery of the head of the Church. Luther judged it "so jocund, so learned, and so ingenious—that is, so entirely Erasmian—that it makes the reader laugh at the vices of the Church, over which every true Christian ought rather to groan." [29] Later, however, his opinion of it rose so high that he would have liked to translate it into German, but feared that he could not do justice to the style.[30]

[29] L. C. ep. 42, to Spalatin, November 1517. Enders, i, 121.

[30] L. C. ep. 130, February 20, 1519. Enders, i, 433. *Cf. Luthers Tischreden*, Weimar, iv, no. 4902, May, 1540. On copies sold in Oxford in 1520 by John Dorne see *Publications of the Oxford Historical Society*, v, 1885, pp. 94, 113, 117.

The Folly of Erasmus

by Hoyt H. Hudson

Through more than four centuries the world has found this book useful. As with so many good things, those who have had most need for it have failed to use it. But as also with many great books, beyond its audience of readers has extended a wide fringe of influence, within which have stood the many who have known that such a book existed, have known, too, that there was something electric in it and that its author transmitted through it, as he did through other of his labors, a spirit whose working sends our minds at once to the parable of the Gospels:

> Whereunto shall I liken the kingdom of God? It is like leaven, which a woman took and hid in three measures of meal, till the whole was leavened.

Yet while this points to the subtle nature of the Erasmian force, and to its manner of diffusion, this gives no account of its direction or content, unless we make bold to press the citation and associate the spirit in question with the kingdom of the parable. We can say, with understatement, that Erasmus is not far from the kingdom; yet to define this last has perplexed our divines. We may hope, with Erasmus, that it is one of the mysteries revealed to the simple and foolish.

Cataloguers put *The Praise of Folly* on the shelf of satire, and with reason; yet we do wrong to make this classification too casually or too absolutely. Satire is directed at an object, or at objects, within the actual view of the satirist. Thus Erasmus makes ridiculous the dishonest and irreligious monks who infested some of the orders. He attacks, both by analysis and by parody, the methods of Biblical interpretation used by scholastics, or by interpreters without Greek or Hebrew. But the vitality of the book does not lie in these jibes or attacks. It owes far more to the comprehensive irony which informs these and other passages where he is pleading, ever so obliquely, for tolerance, for an understanding of human nature, for light on the dark areas of man's world. If the book were, as some have seemed to consider it, an unbroken series of satirical comments, unless it had a positive spirit greater than the keenness or deftness or disinfectant power of these, we could not read it at this late time with edification.

The point seems to be that satirists rarely destroy or appreciably correct the obliquities they attack. If they did, their works would be dull reading indeed. And why should satirists of our time still be shooting at the butts used by Aristophanes, Juvenal, Lucian, and Cervantes? A satirist may succeed in making a person ridiculous, but that is a narrow success which gives him no great claim upon the regard of mankind, particularly of posterity. The real power of great satirists is positive rather than negative. They attract, if at all, by some steady light which burns in them, a light that is benevolent and grateful to the reader—yes, even in Swift, where the style surely rests and invites the spirit as well as the eye. Swift has much humor, as well—another blessing without bitterness. The great satirist lifts the reader to his own plane of clear vision, and wins confidence by reposing in the reader confidence that this vision will be shared. Good satire is an intrigue among honest men, a conspiracy of the candid. But intriguing and conspiring, with a little change of scale, become statesmanship. To return, then, the spirit of Erasmus shows itself in its full power not in overt or direct satire, but rather in overlays of irony and in the positive drive of the whole construction of this eloquent, humane, and finely concatenated speech put in the mouth of Folly. When it is added up, the sum may as well be called criticism as satire. Mary Colum has lately said of criticism that "as an intellectual force it represents a principle through which the world of ideas renews itself, which prunes and trims old ideas to satisfy new ideas and aspirations." Does not *The Praise of Folly* do just this? It is not an irrelevance to notice that this book had been circulating for eighty years in Latin and forty years in English when Shakespeare began to write.

Mrs. Colum goes on: "Purely literary criticism . . . represents, in the work of its highest practitioners, that branch of literature whose most important office is the originating of ideas, the discovery of the circumstances, the foreseeing of the lines that other branches of literature follow." Erasmus does not do all this, and certainly he is not writing purely literary criticism. And yet—there is an old "critical problem" concerning the relation of art and morality, or of art and truth, though the shorter and uglier word may change the problem somewhat. Recently the question has involved art and propaganda; and critics have sought to dissociate the two, to justify or to condemn their copresence, to set up art as pure form, or to transcend the distinction in some other way. In *The Praise of Folly,* one might say, Erasmus did not consider this or any related question. Yet he contributed to thought upon the subject and helped determine the practice of the sixteenth and of later centuries. With him the problem took the form of the relation of classical art, classical poetry and mythology in particular, to the Christian doctrine and life. Can anyone who reads this book doubt where he stands? Yet he never talks about the matter except to make fun, in good Lucianic fashion, of "the gods of the poets," to utter burlesque invocations to the Muses, to speak of Horace (in Horace's own words, to be sure) as "that fat sleek hog from the sty of Epicurus," to call Homer "the father of nonsense," and to quote him in very trivial connections. He was revealing, not stating, that poetry may be read and enjoyed without being treated either as an insidious intoxicant or as the vehicle of sacrosanct wisdom, and that the better a person knows poetry the more fun he can have with it. The reader is aware, long before laying down the book, that Erasmus cares deeply for classical poetry, and that he believes a Christian will be better off for knowing Greek—though he also believes that among unlettered folk will be found some of the best and most admirable Christians. Since both beliefs appear to be borne out by observation, Erasmus may not have been wrong, though the flat statement sounds paradoxical.

How did this subtle and complex construction come into being? Let us begin with the document. Μορίας Εγκώμιον, Erasmus's own title for it became in Latinized Greek *Moriae Encomium,* and in Latin *Stultitiae Laus.* It would have been more accurate and informing if our early translators had closely followed the Greek and had brought the book into English as "Folly's Eulogy," or "The Panegyric of Folly." An encomium (or encomion) is a eulogy or panegryric, a species of the genus oration. It is a set speech giving and asking praise of its subject, and in the orthodox tradition of serious rhetoric its subject is a person, living or dead. A rhetorical game grew up, as we may learn from Erasmus himself, in which one might compose a eulogy of one of the gods, of a character in Homer, or even of the ass; one might pronounce a panegyric upon baldness, or write in praise of darkness, or of nothing. Erasmus also refers to this work as a "declamation," another rhetorical term, with the special suggestion that the speech was thought of as an academic one, or as a "show piece," for no particular occasion. Since the audience is once addressed as *Viri,* and the speaker is wearing an academic gown, we are led to think that Erasmus had in mind a gathering in a college hall, before which a "senior sophister," or even a distinguished visiting scholar, might well appear with a learned declamation.

The topics for composing a eulogy upon a man were set forth in the standard books of instruction for speakers and writers, beginning with Aristotle's *Rhetoric.* The doctrine was that the speaker should begin with a man's ancestry and family, and find something notable there; perhaps even the country or city of his birth would lend evidence of his merit; his upbringing and education would be canvassed for similar evidence; and then one passed on to his achievements, his virtues, his public honors, and so on. Somewhere along the line, the speaker might magnify the man's friends and associates, or the people who served him, in order to borrow thence some glory. Each circumstance was not only mentioned but also amplified—aggravated, if you like. Thus if a man was descended from kings or nobles, of course he partook of their noble and royal qualities; if he came of humble stock, his own virtue was the greater for having climbed above the common run without the advantage of high birth. If one eulogized, as a *jeu d'esprit,* such a thing as mud (and *Luti Encomium* by M. Antonius Majoragius is extant), one might treat the matter of parentage fancifully, saying that the parents of mud are those two most serviceable and ancient of all creatures, water and earth. All of this lore, the reader of *The Praise of Folly* finds, was known to Erasmus and put to use by Folly.

There are other traditions lying back of the book and flowing through it to modern times. They belong in our picture, however briefly they must be dismissed here. One is the tradition of "fool literature," of which the great seamark is the *Narrenschiff*—"Ship of Fools"—which Sebastian Brant, a Strasburg inn-keeper's son who had become a learned lawyer, composed in his native Swabian dialect and published in 1494. In easy verses Brant characterizes 112 kinds of fools who journeyed aboard his imagined ship. *Narrenschiff* became *Stultifera Navis* when it was translated into Latin in 1497, and thus it circulated widely through Europe. Then Badius Ascensius, a Flemish friend of Erasmus's, believing that Brant had not allowed enough women on board his boat, wrote an enlarged version, with six more ships provided for female fools. This work by Badius was in Latin, but it was translated into French at once by a translator who further enlarged it. And so it went. *Narrenschiff* came to people who could read only English in two versions published in the same year, 1509. One, a prose rendering of the French enlargement of Badius's translation and enlargement of Brant, was made by a young man named Henry Watson. The other, more successful and more widely read, was Alexander Barclay's *Ship of Folys of the World,* "translated out of Laten, Frenche and Doche." This is rhymed in very halting verses and stanzas, and by its author's own avowal keeps no close adherence to any of his several originals. Barclay had discovered some fools in England who fell under none of the many classes described by Continental authorities upon the subject.

At any rate, it is interesting to remember that while Erasmus, who knew his Brant in Latin and perhaps in one or two other tongues as well, rode over the Alps from Italy, meditating upon folly, and while at the house of Thomas More, suffering from lumbago, he wrote out the fruits of his meditation, Henry Watson and Alexander Barclay were also engrossed with their own compilations upon the same subject. The presses of Henry Pynson and Wynkyn de Worde in London were thumping, proof was being read, printers were justifying forms and hanging up freshly-printed sheets to dry—all occupied with folly. Erasmus's own book was put into type two years later, 1511, and captivated literate Europe.

A still more important influence in shaping this book was a favorite author of Erasmus's, Lucian. We need learn no other names for this great humorist, since he has come down as plain Lucian, though sometimes given the addition, "of Samasota," the town on the Euphrates river where he was born. He was a Syrian of late Rome, dying about A.D. 200, and so much the cosmopolitan that he seems never to have stayed long in one place, but knew the cities of Asia Minor, Greece, Italy, Egypt, and even Gaul. He left some eighty-five works in Greek prose, mostly short and in the form of eulogies, lectures, monologues, essays, narratives, and, above all, dialogues. The world knows best his *Dialogues of the Gods, Dialogues of Courtesans,* and *Dialogues of the Dead*; and possibly with these should be named his *True History,* an account of his travels "from the Pillars of Hercules into the Western Ocean," including a visit to Elysium and conversations with the shades of philosophers and heroes, the whole a parody of the old historians, travel-writers, and poets. Lucian also wrote the story of the golden ass, which we know better in the telling of Apuleius, his contemporary. Almost every sort of literary treatment except the orthodox poetic one of idealized representation we find in Lucian. From what is nowadays called "stark realism" through scurrility, irony, burlesque, parody, satire, the mock-heroic, to fantasy, here is God's plenty.

Lucian was a favorite with men of the Renaissance, and six of his dialogues had been put into type at Rome in or by 1472. There were thirty-five publications of parts of his work, either in the original or translated into Latin, before 1500. Aldus issued his *Opera* at Venice in 1503, with a title-page bearing four lines in Greek, "Lucian to his Book," which have been translated thus:

> These are the works of Lucian, who knew that folly is of ancient birth, and that what seems wise to some men appears ridiculous to others; there is no common judgment in men, but what you admire others will laugh at.

These are sentiments we find expressed also by Erasmus's Folly. By 1505 Erasmus and Thomas More, who may have discovered this author before Erasmus did, were at work translating dialogues by Lucian into Latin, and thirty-two of their versions (of which twenty-

eight were by Erasmus) were printed by Badius in Paris, 1506. On the
title-page of this work by an ancient scoffer it was recorded that the
translator was *nuper sacri theologiae laurea decorato,* that is, Erasmus, had "recently been honored with the degree of Doctor of Sacred
Theology" by the University of Turin.

Later Erasmus was to publish translations of seven more pieces by
Lucian, and to write his own colloquies, some of which follow closely
the models set by the old Syrian. But enough has been said, though
more is available, to prove him a Lucianist. Some years after he had
published *The Praise of Folly* he wrote to a friend that it was Thomas
More's fondness for wit and fun, "and especially for Lucian," that
prompted him to write this book. The early part is Lucianic in its
scoffing at the gods of mythology; and farther on Erasmus borrows
from Lucian the view of the world as seen from heaven or from
a great height, the world compared to a stage, and other devices. The
reader who has not had time for Lucian may yet encounter here, and
probably enjoy, the Lucianic irony. It is less obviously benevolent
than Socratic irony. It is likely to hold itself, as well as other things,
lightly. It cuts more than one way. The reader may also catch something of Lucian's bounteous fluency, his comprehensiveness, by virtue
of which he seems to be driving several horses at once, but seems also
to miss nothing of the landscape or the crowd through which he drives.
He is likely to be joking or emitting puns to boot. This quality we
know better, perhaps, in Rabelais, who was both a Lucianist and an
Erasmian.

From all the Lucianic bounty we might single out one somewhat
submerged detail, which we may call "learned parody." Not in
Lucian alone, but everywhere in the body of classical and modern
literature, we find fun generated out of the very modes and techniques
of learning itself. This fun cannot be made by one who is himself innocent of scholarship. It is no game for either the plain, blunt man or
the literary dilettante. The audience, too, must have had some converse
with the learned world. The author must have gone far enough in some
discipline to handle easily the technical terms and to pursue the most
highly approved methods, even though he intends to pursue them *ad
absurdum* as rapidly as possible. Some beginning of this kind of thing
we find in Aristophanes; another sort of beginning we find among the
Sophists, but they sought admiration rather than amusement or satire
when they composed elaborate and closely-knit arguments in support
of paradoxes, or worse. They could "make the worse appear the better
cause" and were proud to show off their ability. Readers of Plato's
Phaedrus have encountered *tours de force* of this kind. Then through
the mock-eulogies we have spoken of, and Lucianic burlesque, we ar-
rive at the learned parody of the Renaissance in such a work as *The
Praise of Folly* or *The Epistles of Obscure Men* (1516–17), though

this last uses other modes as well and is by way of being a hoax. From a later age we get that excellent specimen, *The Art of Sinking* (1728) by Pope or by Pope and his friends. Even Lamb's "Dissertation upon Roast Pig" partakes of this tradition.

One device which cannot be dissociated from learned parody is the turning of a method or practice against itself. Thus Bishop John Jewel, the chief ornament of the English church before Hooker, as a young university lecturer composed and delivered an oration against rhetoric in which he exemplified rhetorical figures and modes in the course of ridiculing their use. Ben Jonson wrote "A Fit of Rhyme against Rhyme." We find this device in Erasmus, of course. Early in the eulogy he begins sprinkling in Greek words and phrases, and continues doing so to the end. But also early in it he singles out as one of the bad habits of modern rhetoricians this sprinkling of Greek words and phrases in their Latin compositions; he admits that he copies them. They do so, he says, to show that they are bilingual—a distinction shared by the horseleech. They also seek to confuse and overawe their readers. Then he goes on with the practice. He scoffs at modern authors for using cryptic words, usually in a foreign tongue, as titles of their books; yet his own book bears two words of Greek as a title. But an account of all his devices of learned parody would summarize much of the book; and the topic leads to larger considerations of scholarly self-consciousness and self-criticism which belong with our final estimate of the Erasmian spirit.

A closer study of what literature Erasmus had freshly in mind when Folly began speaking would bring us to Aristophanes and Horace. The running battle she maintains with the Stoics had a model in Horace's satires and epistles. Much of the middle third of *The Praise of Folly* seems to have been suggested by Satire II, iii, which Pope later drew upon. The perfect wise man of the Stoics (Section 14) appears briefly at the end of Horace's first epistle. These details we cannot pursue. As an influence of a different sort, however, we must mention Erasmus's interest in the verities of Christian doctrine, his belief that the church had fallen away from the mind of its founder and early apostles. With this zeal for what he called "the philosophy of Christ" went an acceptance, in some measure, of the Christianized Platonism which had been arrived at by some of the Italian thinkers of the preceding generation. These modes of thought and feeling had already manifested themselves in England, to bear fruit especially in the teaching and preaching of John Colet, Dean of St. Paul's, whom both Erasmus and More admired. Thus as he rode from Italy and thought about England, it was not folly alone that engaged his mind, or his happy remembrance of the facetious Thomas More; it was also his deepest fears and hopes, his most serious thoughts, and greatest admirations, connected with religion and learning.

Let us get back to the document. Folly appears in the pulpit, a young woman, as Holbein saw her, fresh and piquant. She wears the gown of a scholar but her own cap, which has two long peaks so placed and shaped as to suggest that they are designed to cover ass's ears, and each ending in a knob—the bells of the jester. She begins a eulogy of herself, complaining at the ingratitude which men have shown; for while they have eulogized trivial objects and bad men, not one has had the grace to eulogize Folly, to whom they owe so much. Well, blow your own horn, she says, if no one will blow it for you. She knows she is good. Every circumstance—her parentage, her birthplace, her companions, the effects of her presence, the sorry spectacle of the wise men who shun her, the happiness of fools, the power she wields— everything conduces to enhance her attractions and magnify her great- ness. She turns to show how different classes of men, and all women, depend upon folly for their happiness. The reader is swept along. He has seen something of the follies of the world, and recognizes the portraits. This is not mere fooling. Again and again Folly scores a palpable hit.

One has an uneasy consciousness, to be sure, that she is breaking the rules. She takes special advantage of the fact that some words have two or more meanings; and when they do not have two meanings, in the stricter sense, they have two or more sets of connotations, and Folly knows how to skip among these, cutting across lots and leaving heads in a whirl. "There's nothing either good or bad, but thinking makes it so." Folly said it before Shakespeare, in her own way; she said that there is no truth of things, but only opinions about them. Aristotle had gravely set down in his *Rhetoric* this advice to the eulogist:

> For the purposes of praise or blame, the speaker may identify a man's actual qualities with qualities bordering on them. Thus a cautious man may be represented as cold and designing, a simpleton as good-natured, a callous man as easy-going. And so in each case we may substitute one of the collateral terms, always leaning toward the best; terming the choleric and passionate man, for instance, a plain-dealer, and the arrogant man superb and dignified. . . . Thus the rash man may be described as courageous, and the spendthrift as liberal; for so it will seem to the crowd, and meanwhile a false inference can be drawn from the man's motive.

Folly knows this device, whether to use it or to expose it. The proverbs of the folk are at her tongue's end, and all seem to favor her. She also knows the approved method of literary and Biblical exegesis. Homer, Horace, and Cicero are on her side. But lest among Christians these authors have no credit, she also shows from Holy Writ that folly is honorable. Solomon and St. Paul are her best witnesses. David, Jeremiah, and Ecclesiasticus have dropped expressions which she can interpret to her purpose. Even our Lord seemed to favor the simple as against those the world calls wise. His followers are not ashamed to be called sheep, and the constant practice of the Holy Scriptures is to draw metaphors from the more innocent and perhaps more foolish animals.

Along with her equivocations, her absurdities, her high selectivity, Folly offers much that is straight satire of what the reader is glad to see satirized. Worse than this, more disturbing, that is, to one who is under the illusion that the book is the *jeu d'esprit* it pretends to be, Folly again and again talks the soundest of sense or shows a flash of poetic insight that goes beyond what even the best of good sense can ordinarily compass. The power of illusion to enhance daily life, the strength of meekness and the beauty of humility, the sadness of the human lot—these are realized in symbols or illuminated by an oblique light. As with other great books, this seems to be many books. Carlyle's "clothes philosophy" is here. Strip the clothes from the actors, says Folly, and there will be no play. See the contradiction between the king's clothes, crown, and sceptre, and the man whom they disguise. Thackeray's *Book of Snobs* is suggested, as is Bunyan's picture of Vanity Fair. Pope's clear assertion of man's duty to remain in his station and to study what is proper to him is here also. The animals are happy, says Folly, because each follows his proper nature; man alone attempts the preposterous. Mark Twain's "poor damned human race" is very much here. Sir William Temple wrote a good sentence: "When all is done, humane life is, at the greatest and the best, but like a froward child, that must be played with and humoured a little to keep it quiet, till it falls asleep, and then the care is over." Folly said as much in several ways, and at times with almost the same cadence. Something of Rabelais is in the book; something of Swift. "The man from Mars," who sees life on earth clearly and speaks the inconvenient truth about it, is here; Folly calls him "a man dropped down from the sky." The method of Defoe's *Shortest Way with Dissenters* is the method of Folly, or at least of Erasmus. We have, in a word, a compendium of satires and comedies, with no one of them developed at full length.

Not even the figure of Folly is consistently or clearly imagined. An author who was more of a poet than Erasmus would have given her at once more depth, definition, and integrity. As one scholar has observed, in the early part of the speech she seems to be the wicked folly of Christian and Hebrew morality; farther on she embodies a conception gained from the good-natured but shrewd fool of the courts; and finally (though not in the peroration) she becomes Christian folly, a conception having kinship with the tradition and doctrine of St. Francis of Assisi. Holbein's rosy demoiselle is an inadequate figure, and could not possibly have delivered this speech. Interestingly enough, the engraver for the Leyden edition (1703) changed the face and figure, making Folly middle-aged and somewhat battered in appearance. We may know a great deal about folly when we finish the book, but we should not recognize Folly if we met her on the street. Many a reader, too, has gone over *The Praise of Folly* in an edition without Holbein's sketches and has never even pictured the goddess at the desk or the fool gaping at her discourse. Translators have blurred the small amount of dramatic circumstance which is provided. And while a feigned speech is as much a piece of fiction as any other feigned action, a book like this, which is nothing but a speech, can hardly be completely poetic. That it is a public address, constructed on obvious rhetorical lines, harms it as a poetic or fictional creation. "Dramatic monologues" as poets write them give more of the interior of their speakers, and take their form, too, from an inner necessity of character and its expression.

Yet although Erasmus was an imperfect dramatist, he was, as has been suggested, a great critic. The mordant power of this book is his own, elevated and caught at the top of its form. With all his faults, his cowardice, some would say, and his exhibitions of pettiness—but these are not so many as the phrase suggests—Erasmus seems to have maintained a consistency in his work and life, so that these join to display a spirit which has given heart and hope to his colleagues in scholarship, to all the liberal-minded, in fact, in all countries and in all times since his own. One who does no more than read this one little book of his finds that broad statement credible. Yet it is an easy book to misread. And one leading suggestion of the pages which follow is that while *The Praise of Folly* is an authentic expression of the essential Erasmian spirit, we do wrong to take Folly herself as the author's accredited representative, except in a few passages—and in those he rather forgets that Folly is speaking.

To make clearer this apparently confused view is a nice problem in literary interpretation. We may be helped by analyzing another, more familiar, problem in the same field. Consider the farewell speech of Polonius to Laertes in *Hamlet*—the "few precepts" which the young man going away to the University is to remember. "Be thou familiar, but by no means vulgar." "Give every man thine ear, but few thy voice." "Neither a borrower nor a lender be." And so on, up to this pitch:

> This above all: to thine own self be true;
> And it must follow, as the night the day,
> Thou canst not then be false to any man.

This has been read by millions, and the reading of it, or the effect of it, has varied considerably. Let us suppose that one reader believes that good literature is full of well-phrased sentiments which may be of profit to life and conduct. He will take the speech much as we imagine Polonius hoped Laertes would take it. He believes it, in other words, partly because it sounds like good sense, partly because the spectacle of an aged father saying farewell to his son breaks down or prevents resistance to belief, partly because, knowing Shakespeare to be a great author, the reader infers that what he writes in the form of direct advice will be sound. This reader may even go so far as to quote the concluding three lines in moral exhortations. In general, he ignores entirely the dramatic form of *Hamlet*; if he is conscious of it, he may take the position that even a character in a play may express valuable truths.

For our second reader, let us take one at an opposite extreme. This one knows something about Shakespeare, and the history of the stage and of literature. He judges, from other circumstances of the play, that Shakespeare did not intend Polonius to seem wise or prudent but rather as senile and slightly foolish. Hamlet himself seems to take this view. This reader knows that Shakespeare frequently parodied or satirized common literary or dramatic conventions. In *Midsummer Night's Dream* he burlesqued plays put on by groups of tradesmen. So this reader decides that here Shakespeare is making fun of the whole matter of a father's advice to his son, and he reads Polonius's speech as a parody on such farewell speeches, but one which might well have been produced by such a doting old gaffer as Polonius. He does not believe the speech at all, but he believes it is consistent with the character of Polonius and with the purpose of the dramatist. This is a highly sophisticated reading, just as the first reader's was a naïve one.

A third reader may also find the speech proper to the character of Polonius, but he may judge that since the speaker is represented as being the principal counsellor of the king of Denmark and with much experience of life, he is not altogether a fool; his speech will show some shrewdness, some worldly wisdom, some pompousness and windiness, perhaps; but it is by no means a burlesque of such things. This interpreter will not take it seriously as a guide of life, though he may find sayings in it which seem to hit off with great exactness what appear to be sound rules of conduct. This reader is sophisticated also, but in this interpretation he might be called primarily reasonable.

Yet it is possible to conceive of a reader who stands on another level of reading entirely, a level on which the attitude toward this particular speech becomes a very minor matter. We might call the interpretation at this level a concrete one, by way of distinguishing it from all the others, which alike tended to be abstract. Our fourth reader (though any other, by grace or discipline, may also stand on this level) is likely not to give any interpretation to this particular speech except while he reads, or just after he reads, the entire play. He finds the whole not only more important than the parts, but also more absorbing. He arrives at his conception of the whole, you may say, by reading or hearing the parts, perhaps also by the use of much commentary and analysis.

Even so, once the conception is present, his reading of any particular speech is always tangential to or conditional upon it. It is not merely an intellectual structure, to be diagrammed and fixed, but it is experiential. That is the reason he wishes to go over the whole before discussing this speech. Sophistication, or the control of attitudes by a purposive manipulation of somewhat isolated pieces of knowledge, gives way to imagination, which works to fuse all experience—even the experience of being sophisticated and that of being reasonable— into a unity. Our reader sees the play, it must be, as a world, a universe, to be entered. Much as he may like to enter it, he cannot very well carry pieces out of it. Of what we ordinarily call the universe, whose form and limits, whose oneness, even, we cannot see, we usually say that we might understand the whole if we could fully understand a single object in it. Yet this would be true only if we had a sense of the whole, or of wholeness, to begin with. The world given us in a poetic work has the great advantage that it presents this sense of wholeness vividly. Just how particular persons who read concretely would interpret Polonius's speech, these brief remarks do not divulge. To go on in this direction would be to write an essay on *Hamlet*.

The example serves to show varieties and levels of interpretation. Remembering that *The Praise of Folly* is not a consummated poetic fiction, we cannot look to it for a world of its own; yet an interesting analogy will appear, and here also we must strive toward a concrete reading. Some keys to interpretation are plainly inadequate. This might be suggested, for instance: since Erasmus puts his discourse in the mouth of Folly, he intends it all to be foolishness; none of it is to be taken seriously, except as a dramatic presentation of what is foolish. This would indeed result in a naïve reading, and anyone capable of reading the book at all finds at once that the key does not fit. There is almost no straight or mere foolishness in it. Folly may be arguing that as a baby she was better off than was Jupiter as a baby, for he was nursed by a she-goat, whereas she was nursed by two lovely nymphs, Drunkenness and Idleness; but she presents this in beautifully correct sentences in its exact place in a well-planned progression. Farther along, when she tells the duties of a king and the dangers of his position, she talks as gravely as any philosopher. We look for a better key. We know the proverb, as does Folly, "Children and fools sometimes speak the truth." This suggests that while there will be nonsense in the oration, there will be flashes of wisdom much as we find in the parts of the fools in Shakespeare. There are such flashes, but the whole is not to be described in this manner. There are wholly grave sections of considerable length, suggesting Shakespeare's kings and counsellors rather than his fools. There is learned parody, and serious Biblical criticism. Above all, there is a beautiful orderliness and a rising movement quite inconsistent with mere deviation into sense.

Folly herself offers another help toward our interpretation. Referring (in Section 13) to Plato's *Symposium,* she recalls that Alcibiades drew an analogy from the little images of Silenus current at the time, which were ugly when looked at, but which, then opened, were found to contain beautifully carved images of the gods. Folly tells us that we must not be content with the appearances of things but must look for the true interior meaning. (This is inconsistent with what she says elsewhere about the supremacy of opinion, but let that pass.) Pressing this suggestion to the limit, we might be led to say that Erasmus intends Folly really to represent Wisdom. The nonsense or fooling she indulges in, then, is but superficial disguise or a relish, a kind of unbending proper to a wise person. Folly thus becomes a completely "sympathetic" figure, and she has sometimes been so interpreted. Such a key seems more serviceable, indeed, than the others we have tried. Falstaff is a complex character whom we view with mingled emotions but whom, on the whole, we may find sympathetic. We might similarly overlook the inconsistencies of Folly, her suppression of facts—for she rarely dwells upon the consequences of folly—and her defense of bad causes, for the sake of her hatred of pretense, her occasional sweet reasonableness, and her broad sympathies. The main difficulties with the view are that it claims for Folly a consistency which, as has been pointed out, does not exist, and for Erasmus a power of dramatic conception which was denied him. Were Folly really integrated into a character such as this view calls for, she would stand with the few great figures of comic creation in the world's literature. In her own right, as character, she does not so stand. At times she seems to be on the way to become a character; but usually she is a puppet, and at times is forgotten completely by author and reader. So we come back to a divergence between Folly and the book, or between Folly and the author, and say that a concrete reading will involve Erasmus as well as Folly, and even more than Folly.

Both in the author's preface to Thomas More and in the declamation we find stress laid upon the notion that only fools have the privilege of speaking truth without offense. This observation, if dwelt upon, does cut deep into the motives and methods of Erasmus. He has found a device whereby he may say what he wishes to say, speak the truth as he sees it, and still plead immunity. Yet he cannot speak this truth all of the time, or no one will believe it is Folly who is before him. Following this lead, we do well to think of irony. The very writing and issuance of this book was an act of irony on the part of an eminent scholar. He was playfully ironical in connecting it as he did with Thomas More. He was ironical in another way when he said that some people hope to become rich by praying to Erasmus. He was ironical in still another way when he ridiculed the foolish love of fame which keeps scholars at their labors.

Suppose we now premise that Erasmus wishes to show that what is usually accepted as wisdom is not very wise. He will do so by placing much of it in the mouth of Folly but along with this he will put other sentiments which are either below or above the level of ordinary wisdom—for to mundane common sense, what goes beyond or above itself is sheer folly, no less than what falls short of it. The sentiments below the ordinary level will serve to authenticate the speaker as Folly, will provide mirth, and will have a cajoling effect upon the reader, tending to break down categorical boundaries in his mind and to leave him unguarded against other kinds of attack. Sentiments above the ordinary level will be so played up as to emphasize the mediocre nature of worldly wisdom, and will be insinuated into the reader's mind with a novel attractiveness. There is something of an argument *a fortiori* here: if Folly can be as wise as this, what ought wisdom be? Or put more ironically, what men will not accept from the Evangelists and the apostles they will perhaps accept from Folly. We have a key which seems to operate throughout our reading of the eulogy, most of which can be arranged under a scheme based upon this explanation. There will be eddies within the main current, as when Folly herself uses the device of irony with a basis, or fulcrum, in either her own foolishness or her own wisdom, distinguishable from the basis of Erasmus himself. Other eddies will result from mere play of fancy. Yet something is still left over, unexplained by this key, too— principally the gusto, abandon, and joyous release which supply so much of the book's appeal, and perhaps a great part of its real message. The experience of a concrete reading will include the impact of energies as well as the shifting of attitudes and the savor of various kinds of wisdom.

It is time to look again at the document. An interesting passage (Section 17) argues that halfwits and "naturals" such as kings and noblemen used to employ as jesters are really the happiest of men. They are free, says Folly, from tortures of conscience and from fear of death. They play all of the time, and laugh a great deal. Every man, even the coldest, has a soft spot in his heart for these poor souls—except that we must not call them "poor"; Folly does not, but paints them as rich and fortunate. Her position does not represent the wisdom of the world, which may be indulgent toward these innocents but certainly reckons them among the unfortunate. Is what Folly says, then, something less than the wisdom of the world, or more? Taken as a bare argument, it is less. Such halfwits and imbeciles, as Erasmus must have known, have miseries too deep for telling. Even the best of men (such as Thomas More, who had a great liking for natural fools and kept one in his household), though they may be amused or interested by the spectacle of such people, are likely at the same time to feel a kind of pity so deep as to be painful. Others feel mere revulsion. The argument Folly makes, in a word, ignores important facts. But suppose we think of it as being the vehicle for something else, a plea for a sympathetic and understanding attitude toward these unfortunates. Then, we might say, the passage rises above worldly wisdom. It owes something to an old identification of harmless insanity with a sort of possession by divine force. But there is a tenderness in it, such as reminds us of Pope's verses about the poor Indian. Erasmus may be saying what may need to be said, that these dim-sighted souls are human souls and belong within the range of human as well as divine love. "After a life lived out in much jollity," he writes of the halfwits, "with no fear of death, or sense of it, they go straight to the Elysian fields, there to entertain the pious and idle shades with their jests." Erasmus reminds us elsewhere, too, that we are all touched, or liable to be touched, by weakness of mind.

Again, Folly draws in the sharpest of lines the picture of the deluded scholar, seeking to win a vain sort of fame by labors which with the best success in the world can but please a handful of blear-eyed scholars like himself. As a matter of fact, he sets such a man against his happy halfwit for contrast:

> Fancy some pattern of wisdom to put up against him, a man who wore out his whole boyhood and youth in pursuing the learned disciplines. He wasted the best time of life in unintermitted watchings, cares, and studies; and through the remaining part of it he never tasted so much as a tittle of pleasure; always frugal, impecunious, sad, austere; unfair and strict toward himself, morose and unamiable to others; afflicted by pallor, leanness, invalidism, sore eyes, and premature old age and white hair; dying before his appointed day.

Except for the phrase, "morose and unamiable to others," that is an excellent self-portrait. Erasmus spoke from an experience that was not without bitterness. What shall we say, then? By this condemnation of scholarly devotion in the mouth of Folly, does he mean really to condemn it? If so, then why did he, after the age of forty-three at which he wrote this book, go on to perform as prodigious and exacting labors of editorial scholarship as the world has known, not only preparing what was in effect the *editio princeps* of the Greek New Testament, with his own translation, notes, and carefully wrought paraphrase, but editing also the works of St. Chrysostom, St. Jerome, and several other fathers of the church? No, what Folly says hits pretty well the wisdom of the world. Erasmus's own labors are the comment upon it. What we know from this is that he undertook those labors with a clearsighted view of the cost of them. We might even say that he was aware of the folly of them, as judged either by the wisdom of the world or by a higher sort of wisdom which reveals to every man who has it that whatever he may do is in itself vain, and dispensable, yet the soul which he throws into it and the life he builds through it are not necessarily so. Put into other terms, except God build the house, they labor in vain that build it. On the mundane level, also, we notice that the temper of Erasmus did not accord with that of Folly's despised scholar. A favorite word with him was *festivus*—festive, companionable. He refused to allow his scholarship to kill his humanity. And thus Folly's gird has point, even as used by her; the halfwit is understandably human, all too human, while the scholar may verge toward something inhuman or anti-human.

Finally, there is the whole matter of Folly's treatment of the church and of Christian doctrine. The subject is so large that we are confined to a few general observations. Erasmus lived and died as a son of the church, suspected, it is true, of heresies, and even charged with them by many intelligent churchmen. He was hated more bitterly, however, by some of the Protestant Reformers, in that while he seemed to be saying so much they agreed with, he would not take the firm, bold action they believed the hour demanded. In this book we find much that bespeaks the Reformer rather than the orthodox churchman. The truth is that one widely circulated modern edition of Kennett's translation of *The Praise of Folly* was issued by a free-thinking publisher as ammunition in his war against Christianity. In his "Publisher's Preface" he made a long quotation from Folly, beginning, "It is observable that the Christian Religion seems to have some relation to Folly, and no alliance at all with Wisdom," with pleased assent, thereby writing himself down *stultissimum*. He himself wrote: "From the serene Citadel of Truth, armed with the weapons of reason and satire, Erasmus has in this work severely bombarded the strongholds of Faith." But Erasmus, we may flatly say, was interested in defending and arming the strongholds of faith. In Folly's attacks on churchmen she does not stand at the level of worldly wisdom, which in general approves those whom she attacks. Neither, except in moments by the way, is she speaking nonsense. Every attack is precisely against following in the spiritual kingdom the standards and practices that prevail in worldly, carnal affairs. Amid all Folly's shifts and tergiversations, Erasmus never implies that Christianity has more to learn than it has to teach. From one point of view, the church's folly has been that it has gone to school to the world; from another point of view, its folly is its glory.

Yet Folly's freedom with sacred names and texts has shocked many a reverent believer; and in his own time Erasmus was coupled with Lucian as an atheistical scoffer. This freedom, however, is itself a manifestation of that *festivitas* which Erasmus found fully accordant with reverence. One does not hurt the sacred truth by citing it in the mouth of Folly so much as one hurts it by disavowing it in one's life, or using it as a pretext for actions which, though serious and grave enough, are plainly hostile to good feeling and fundamental decency. One's faith may indeed be so real, so present, and so homely that one jests with and about it, as if it were a friend or brother. Erasmus believed that Christianity could be at home in a world of culture as well as in a religious community or among fishers and mechanics. On the other hand, the man of culture would be a fool if his cultivation carried him to the point where he lost touch with the simplicities of the Gospel which are akin to the simplicities of the unlettered human heart, even to those of dumb animals. The paradox here is as inevitable as that other paradox which Folly does not quote but which underlies much of what she says: "For whosoever will save his life shall lose it; and whosoever will lose his life for my sake shall find it."

For a more complete appreciation of Erasmus himself, we need at least to read his *Colloquies* and his *Enchiridion*. Yet the present work, as we have seen with the help of little drawn from outside it, tells us much. Though it contains sad pictures of weakness and misery, it does not tell us to laugh that we may not weep; rather it tells us to weep and to laugh in humility, "as unto the Lord," with a sense of the transience of joy and tears. It suggests that there is a simplicity which embraces and transcends complexity. The divided mind, the conflict of the soul, need not be self-destructive. Although the deepest understanding may not bring such experiences to harmony, or the play of consciousness give them a musical setting, these spiritual powers can at least place them in some degree of esthetic distance and relate them intelligibly to a pattern not quite crazy. At the more customary levels of experience, this book bids us hold our convictions with some lightness, and to add grace to life. Our best work will be done in a critical spirit, which turns upon ourselves and itself the same keen gaze and feasting irony with which it views the world. We like to think that some such spirit informs our universities. But it belongs also to this spirit not to talk about itself. Perhaps too much has been said already.

Before leaving the subject, however, we must give a hearing to the other side. Rare and precious as may be this phlogiston, it is not, we are told, a fuel for the engines of action. A Chinese philosophy resulted in a static China. Academic scepticism unfits a man for the tasks of life, which call rather for the uncritical mind and unhampered will. The answer is perhaps threefold, in part a denial with counter-charge, in part an admission, and in part an amendment. A flat denial, even in part, is the weakest of these. It is indeed true, as has been pointed out, that Socrates would make a bad member of a fire department, were he to answer a fire-call by beginning a dialogue upon whether the burning house is worth saving. Yet it is also fair to say, and needs no insistence, that practical men of undivided will often make a terrible mess of what are supposed to be practical affairs, and seem to go on making such messes either until other practical men, single-minded toward other ends, halt them, or until there is an influx of the critical spirit into some party to the situation. Not every call to action is as immediately urgent as a fire-alarm; and men touched by Erasmian folly—and Abraham Lincoln was one of them—have sometimes planned and controlled and executed palpable tasks. Even Folly admits that Marcus Aurelius was a good emperor. Thomas More—and this book is his, we find, as well as Erasmus's—was a wise and active parliamentarian, diplomat, lawyer, and Lord Chancellor.

Yet we may admit that in emergencies the Erasmian sometimes cuts a poor figure. Erasmus was a pacifist, and his folly seems to unfit men for whole-hearted participation in war. If a man cannot take his place in battle-line when necessity arises, most would say, then there is something fundamentally wrong with him. It is not an adequate answer to say that he represents the civilization which the battle defends. It is not adequate to plead specialization—*non omnia possumus omnes*. It is not adequate to say that he follows the counsel of Plato, to step into a doorway when the storm grows too fierce. On the other hand, one can testify that many a man of Erasmian spirit has gone forth to fight, perhaps not whole-heartedly believing in the complete righteousness of his cause, or even of his action, yet with motives strong enough to make him as good a soldier as the next man. It is certainly possible for one to be willing to die for a cause in which one does not wholly believe. Men die for such causes every day, not always by compulsion. And if, on the other hand, an Erasmian does refuse to fight with carnal weapons, it is just as likely that his refusal, in turn, does not represent what the world would call a whole-hearted action. The relation of the Erasmian spirit to democracy is a subject in itself; but it must occur to anyone at this point that democracies, as states, have proceeded on what we have seen to be the Erasmian principle in individuals. That is, the democratic belief is that a state can exist and be strong without being totalitarian; that it can endure considerable divisions of sentiment within it, and that it can even protect the right of individual conscience without paralyzing the national will.

The concept of emergency, or crisis, comes at times to loom large in our consciousness, and with reason. Yet unless it is to swell and involve all other concepts, there is place for the Erasmian spirit; and if it so extinguishes all else, the Erasmian, at worst, will be but a little less vital than the single-minded man of action. When the Duke of Norfolk pleaded with Thomas More to go along with the Act of Supremacy, warning him that his contumacy might cost him his head, More listened patiently and then said: "Is that all, my Lord? Then in good faith there is no more difference between your Grace and me, but that I shall die today and you tomorrow."

The best in a corrupted form is the worst of all. The degraded Erasmian is the shifty, accommodating Pyrrhonist, sceptical of all except his own kind of scepticism. Irony, in him, becomes cynicism; wit becomes flippancy; and his criticism of life adds up to an avoidance of responsibility. In this he is as far from Erasmus as he is from John Wesley or Julius Caesar. In the present book, one decisive distinction between Folly and the author is that Folly is at times cynical, Erasmus is not. For the rest, what Erasmus did has somehow survived and gone on working. What men of his spirit did and said and wrote has survived to exert a modicum of force in the world. Wars, conquests, and revolutions have not quite extinguished this spirit, and have not made it seem less of a blessing.

The Praise of Folly and Its Background

by Leonard F. Dean

I

The Praise of Folly presents an interesting problem in reading. Like many ironical works, it has been taken too solemnly by some readers, and too lightly by others. It puzzled and offended Martin van Dorp, a conservative professor of theology at Louvain University. "You should know," he wrote earnestly to Erasmus in 1514, "that your *Moria* has excited a great disturbance even among those who were formerly your most devoted admirers. . . . It is not for me to advise, but I humbly believe that you can easily make everything right by composing and publishing in reply to Folly, a Praise of Wisdom." [1] That Erasmus was exasperated is suggested by his comment to Sir Thomas More: "I can't imagine what has got into Dorp's head. Well, this is what theology does to a person." [2] Nevertheless, both Erasmus and More replied to Dorp. One defense was the conventional assertion that the piece should not be taken seriously. "I was laid up at More's house for a few days with the lumbago on my return from Italy," Erasmus explains carefully, "and since my books were not at hand, and since I was too sick to do any serious work, I amused and distracted myself by composing a praise of folly. Some friends professed to like the parts they saw and urged me to complete it, which I did in seven days—altogether too long a time, of course, to spend on such a subject. Then the same friends contrived to have the book published in France." But Erasmus was perfectly aware that this rather half-hearted account would not do, so he went on to an explanation of what ought to have been obvious.

---

[1] *Opus Epistolarum*, ed. P. S. Allen (Oxford, 1906–), Ep. 304; *The Epistles of Erasmus*, tr. F. M. Nichols (London, 1901–18), Ep. 304. Hereafter cited as Allen and Nichols.

[2] Allen, Ep. 412; Nichols, Ep. 399.

"The ideas in *The Praise of Folly*," he continues painfully, "are exactly the same as those in my other essays, but here they are presented ironically (*via diversa*). In the *Enchiridion* I gave a straightforward description of the Christian way of life. *The Education of a Christian Prince* is a plain account of how a ruler should be trained. Now in *The Praise of Folly*, under the pretext of a eulogy, I approach obliquely the same ideas that I elsewhere have presented directly." [3]

No one today, presumably, would make Martin van Dorp's mistake of taking literally the ironical statements in *The Praise of Folly*. The modern mistake is either to dismiss the book as another straddling utterance by a man who, compared to the unironical Luther, never took a stand, or to interpret the irony as a kind of mildly pleasant jesting which has lost whatever serious point it may have had. A writer in *The London Times Literary Supplement* remarks fairly typically that "The 'Praise of Folly' Erasmus spoke of always as a piece of foolishness. He had wished to amuse the world with it. . . . But he had not wished to fire a crusade. . . . Instead of speaking of 'spiritual dynamite' [following Froude] it would be simpler, perhaps, though it would not sound so well, to call the 'Folly' a theological squib. It is a squib which today, perhaps, dances and crackles a little disappointingly. Both in history and in the history of literature the book has its proper place, and will continue to be read. Yet, when we wish to say of it, What a fine piece of literature this is! common honesty plucks us back, and, What a fine piece of journalism, we say, this *was*." [4]

In order to show that these two representative modern interpretations of *The Praise of Folly* are mistaken it is necessary to argue that irony may be serious and that it may be the most direct and accurate mode of expression for complex ideas. For the moment we may remind ourselves simply that in a continued irony several different attitudes are kept in balance to produce a meaning that is larger and in a sense more precise than that produced by a narrowly direct statement. Before continuing with this discussion, it will be useful to review the development of Erasmus as a thinker and writer in order to show the growing complexity of his mind, and to suggest the possibility that irony was finally the most adequate mode of expression for a man of his diverse interests and attitudes.

II

From the beginning of his formal education, Erasmus was concerned with the proper relation of learning and piety. Upon entering the

monastic school at Steyn in 1487, he composed *De contemptu mundi,*
and other conventional religious exercises, but he very soon began to
rebel against a curriculum that seemed to him excessively narrow and
theological. This rebellion appears as a fine youthful enthusiasm for
the classics and for the elegancies of Latin style. He conceived of himself, somewhat melodramatically, as living in the midst of barbarians.
"It is certain," he wrote in 1489, "that in early ages the study of eloquence, as of other arts, was most flourishing, and afterwards, as the
obstinacy of the barbarians increases, it disappeared . . . Our Thalia
was well nigh extinct when our Laurentius and Philelphus by their
admirable erudition saved her from perishing. The books of the former,
which are called *Elegentiae,* will show you with what zeal he exerted
himself both to expose the absurdities of the barbarians and to bring
back into use the observances of orators and poets long covered with
the dust of oblivion." [5] At about this time Erasmus made an epitome
of Valla's *Elegantiae* for school use; it was published in 1529, and followed in 1531 by a revised, authorized version, which became a standard textbook, nearly forty editions appearing within twenty years.
Before he left Steyn in 1492, Erasmus attempted a written defense and
clarification of his rebellious attitude by composing the *Antibarbari* or
Book Against the Barbarians.[6] It was to be an attack on the barbarians
and a eulogy of classical literature, but only the first part has survived.
It was completed by 1495, but withheld from publication because of
its controversial nature, and finally printed for the first time in 1520
in a revised form. The revision had been made at Bologna in 1506–7,
shortly before Erasmus left for England, where *The Praise of Folly*
was written in 1509. It is one of many examples of Erasmus' habit of
reworking older pieces while busy at the same time on new ones, a
habit which helps to account for the unity of his writings.

The *Antibarbari* is a dialogue in which the subject under discussion
is analyzed through speakers with different points of view. A physician,
Jodocus, suggests that the stars are responsible for the deplorable state
of humane learning; William Herman, a friend of the author, attributes it to the general decay of the world; and James Batt, another
friend with humanistic leanings, lays the blame on ignorant monks and
scholastic theologians, who have corrupted the purity of the early
Christian faith and have deliberately kept the people in ignorance of
the classics under the pretext of protecting religion. It follows that reform is possible and can be effected by getting rid of benighted school
teachers and impoverished medieval textbooks. William Conrad, a
practical and conservative mayor, wonders if it is wise to replace the
standard texts with untried classics, which, furthermore, may be an

[5] Allen, Ep. 23; Nichols, Ep. 22.
[6] See Albert Hyma, *The Youth of Erasmus,* Univ. of Mich. Publications in History
and Political Science, X, 1930, Chap. XV and Appendix 3.

immoral influence on young minds. Batt answers by denouncing bigots who attack literature in the name of religion. They write and teach a barbarous Latin style and assert that a knowledge of Greek is heresy. It may be also suspected, continues Batt, that classical poetry is less harmful than the immoral influence of monastic life. Actually, the split between religion and secular learning is needless and unreal: the Church Fathers knew and used the classics; they were pious and critical-minded at the same time. The discussion is extended at this point to include the belief of the mystics that the pure in heart, rather than the learned, will inherit heaven. Did not Christ Himself preach humility and simplicity? What of the ordinary people who are ignorant of syllogisms and fine rhetoric? The first reply is a facetious suggestion that those who wish to enter heaven with the innocent, dumb animals may do so. It is then argued more seriously that there is a distinction between simplicity of heart and simple-mindedness, and that Christ was talking about character rather than intellect. The illiterate and licentious monks are a sufficient illustration of the confusion. Furthermore, the influence of piety is extended by means of learning; a good man who is also educated and eloquent can do more than an untutored person, even a martyr, to spread Christ's word. The argument that Christianity was founded by uneducated fishermen, the Apostles, is also suspect since it is usually no more than an excuse for people nowadays to continue in their own ignorance. The truth is that the Apostles were carefully instructed by Christ, the real father of philosophy; they needed no further secular training. Besides, not all of the Apostles were ignorant to begin with: witness Paul, Peter, John, and James. Our aim should be to combine the religious fervor of Peter, the foremost Apostle, and the learning of Jerome, the foremost Church Father. Here, the mayor interrupts with the objection that the issue has been confused. No one denies that the Apostles possessed divine learning; the subject in question is secular learning acquired through human discipline, and the piety of the Apostles was not the product of study, but of heavenly grace. True, grants Batt rather lamely in conclusion, and all our books are useless without the Holy Spirit, but an occasional visitation, when we are preaching or writing, is preferable to a complete and overwhelming revelation.

The issues presented somewhat crudely in the *Antibarbari* were sharpened for Erasmus by his experiences at the University of Paris, where he entered the College of Montaigu in August of 1495 and took a degree of Bachelor in Theology about two years later. Here, at first hand, he saw grown men arguing with the greatest energy and acuteness about words alone. Could Christ have appeared in the form of a gourd? If so, how could He have preached, performed miracles, and been crucified? Which is the greater crime: to kill a thousand men or to work on Sunday? The sight of this remarkable waste of human abilities helped Erasmus to distinguish more exactly between nominalism and a true, realistic theology. He writes about his experience in a wryly humorous letter to an English friend, Thomas Grey, sometime in 1497.

I, who have always been a primitive Theologian, have begun of late to be a Scotist. . . . We are so immersed in the dreams of your compatriot,—for Scotus, who, like Homer of old, has been adopted by diverse competing countries, is especially claimed by the English as their own,—that we seem as if we should hardly wake up at the voice of Stentor. Then you will say, you are writing this in your sleep. Hush, profane one! thou knowest nothing of theological slumber. There are many that in their sleep not only write, but slander and get drunk, and commit other indiscretions. . . . What if you saw Erasmus sit gaping among those blessed Scotists, while Gryllard is lecturing from his lofty chair? If you observed his contracted brow, his staring eyes, his anxious face, you would say he was another man. They assert that the mysteries of this science cannot be comprehended by one who has any commerce at all with the Muses or with the Graces. If you have touched good letters, you must unlearn what you have learnt; if you have drunk of Helicon, you must get rid of the draught. I do my best to speak nothing in true Latin, nothing elegant or witty, and I seem to make some progress. There is hope that they will acknowledge Erasmus some time or other. . . . Sweet Grey, do not mistake me. I would not have you construe this as directed against theology itself, which, as you know, I have always regarded with special reverence. I have only amused myself in making game of some pseudo-theologians of our time, whose brains are rotten, their language barbarous, their intellects dull, their learning a bed of thorns, their manners rough, their life hypocritical, their talk full of venom, and their hearts as black as ink.[7]

What it meant to be a "primitive theologian" was made clearer to Erasmus by John Colet, whom he met at Oxford in October of 1499, during his first visit to England. The two men, both about thirty years old, agreed in condemning scholastic theology. "In your dislike of that sort of neoteric divines, who grow old in mere subtleties and sophistical cavillings, your opinion is entirely my own," Erasmus writes. "In our day, theology, which ought to be at the head of all literature, is mainly studied by persons who from their dulness and lack of sense are scarcely fit for any literature at all. This I say not of learned and honest professors of theology, however. . . ." [8] Colet exemplified the fruitful union of classical and biblical learning that Erasmus had advocated all along. Colet was as eager as the professors at the College of Montaigu to discuss theology, but his aim, unlike

[7] Allen, Ep. 64; Nichols, Ep. 59.
[8] Allen, Ep. 108; Nichols, Ep. 108.

theirs, was to explain the essential meanings of the teaching of Christ
and the Apostles. A conversation between the two men about the
cause of Christ's agony in the garden illustrates the Englishman's point
of view and method. Erasmus proposed the conventional scholastic
explanation that the agony was a reflection of the natural fear of tor-
ment and death felt by Christ the man. Colet, following Jerome, urged
that such a view was inconsistent with the principle of Christ the
redeemer, who, far from fearing death, sought to die because of His
infinite love for all mankind. His prayer that the cup might pass from
Him, and the drops of bloody sweat wrung from Him in the garden,
were not expressions of fear, but of compassion and sorrow at the
thought of the crime which was to be committed. It was in a continua-
tion of the same mood that He prayed, "Father, forgive them, for they
know not what they do." [9] It became evident, as the discussion was
continued by letter, that Colet was directly opposed to the scholastic
tendency to extract more than one literal sense from biblical texts.
He did not deny that some passages should be interpreted allegorically,
but he did believe that it was uncritical to read into the Scriptures a
variety of literal meanings, for the purpose of argument, that were not
consistent with the total meaning of the whole context. The critic
must first absorb and comprehend the essential spirit of the Bible; in
its light he might then proceed to explicate individual passages, much
as one might attempt to master a secular classic. To the argument
that manifold interpretations are justified in the case of the Bible
because its author was God, who comprehends and expresses all meanings at one and the same time, Colet tended to oppose the point of
view of historical scholarship. His "method," as Allen observes, "raised
the question of the Tradition." The questions to be asked were "not
how mankind would have been born if our first parents had not fallen,
nor whether the wicked continue to sin in hell, but what were the
words of Christ, and by what means these had been preserved to posterity. If the Scriptures were to be treated historically, they must be
studied in their original form, or in the nearest form to that, which
critical scholarship could discover." [10]

The association with Colet seems to have strengthened and guided
Erasmus in several ways. The *Enchiridion Militis Christiani,* or Manual of the Christian Knight, which Erasmus composed in 1501 on his
return to the Continent, and published in 1503, reflects the Englishman's essential piety and justifies the author's characterization of the
essay as a "straightforward description of the Christian way of life."
The Praise of Folly picks up and expands the basic argument of the

---

[9] Allen, Eps. 108–111; see Frederic Seebohm, *The Oxford Reformers* (London,
1896), pp. 116–118.

[10] P. S. Allen, "Erasmus' Services to Learning," *Proc. of the British Academy,* XI
(1925), 357.

Enchiridion, which distinguishes between real and superficial piety. Religious ceremonies, particularly the worship of the saints, are condemned when they do not symbolize sincere righteousness; the only true worship is virtuous behavior. *"The Enchiridion,"* Erasmus explained to Colet in 1504, "was not composed from any display of genius or eloquence, but only for the purpose of correcting the common error of those who make religion consist of ceremonies and an almost Jewish observance of corporeal matters, while they are singularly careless of things that belong to piety." [11] Piety was not to be confused, however, with ignorant mysticism. Erasmus still desired to unite learning and religion, as is indicated by the concluding sentences of the *Enchiridion:* "I hope to disarm some critics who think it is the highest religion to know nothing of good learning. It was not for empty fame or childish pleasure that in my youth I grasped at the polite literature of the ancients, and by late hours gained some slight mastery of Greek and Latin. It has long been my cherished wish to cleanse the Lord's temple of barbarous ignorance, and to adorn it with treasures brought from afar, such as may kindle in generous hearts a warm love for the Scriptures." [12]

There is other evidence from this period that Erasmus had begun to outgrow his youthful delight in the mere elegancies of Latin style. Before leaving England, he had refused Colet's invitation to lecture at Oxford, on the ground that he was unprepared to treat theology. "Neither again," he adds, "did I come here to teach Poetry or Rhetoric. These studies ceased to be agreeable to me when they ceased to be necessary." [13] They were no longer necessary, that is, in the sense that they had been mastered so as to become a part of his unconscious equipment as a writer. There, properly subordinated, they helped to increase the effectiveness of his message, as *The Praise of Folly* most clearly demonstrates. A further sign of his growing maturity in this respect and of his surer sense of direction as a scholar, is his turning from Latin to Greek, which he began to study seriously at about this time. "Latin erudition, however ample, is crippled and imperfect without Greek," he wrote in 1501, and he saw that this was particularly true for one who wished as he now did to edit, translate, and interpret the Scriptures and the Church Fathers. "I see that it is mere madness to touch with a finger that principal part of theology, which treats of divine mysteries, without being furnished with the apparatus of Greek, when those who translated the sacred books have, with all their scrupulosity, so rendered the Greek figures of speech that not even the primary sense, which our theologians call 'the literal,' can be per-

[11] Allen, Ep. 181; Nichols, Ep. 180.
[12] Allen, Ep. 164; translated by Allen, "Erasmus' Services to Learning," p. 357.
[13] Allen, Ep. 108; Nichols, Ep. 108.

ceived by those who do not know Greek." [14] Still clearer and more forceful are the arguments by Erasmus in his preface to Valla's *Notes on the New Testament*. Erasmus had found a manuscript of this un-published textual criticism of the Vulgate and had printed it in 1505. He is well aware, he writes, that it will shock many people, and espe-cially the conservative theologians who most need to profit by it. They will assert that a grammarian has no right to meddle with theology. But when theologians argue about the language of the Scriptures—as they always do, are they not for the moment grammarians? If the problem is grammatical, let it be called by its right name, and treated openly and in a scholarly fashion. "What crime is it in Valla, if after collating some ancient and correct Greek copies, he has noted in the New Testament, which is derived from the Greek, some passages which either differ from our version or seem to be ineptly rendered owing to a passing want of vigilance in the translator, or are expressed more significantly in the Greek; or finally if it appears that some thing in our text is corrupt?" Perhaps it will be answered that it is improper and dangerous to alter the Holy Scriptures, wherein even the smallest points possess hidden meanings. "This only shows how wrong it is to corrupt them, and how diligently what has been altered by ignorance ought to be corrected by the learned." To the further objection "that the old interpreters, skilled in three tongues, have already unfolded the matter as far as is necessary," I answer, first, that "I had rather see with my own eyes than with those of others; and in the next place, much as they have said, they have left much to be said by poster-ity . . ." [15] Stimulated by Valla's essay and by a second visit to Colet, Erasmus began a Latin version of the New Testament, which he com-pleted in manuscript form, except for Acts and Revelations, by 1506. Ten years later, after many revisions, it was printed with a Greek edition and notes, and thereafter re-edited four times. At the same time he began his editorial work on the writings of the Church Fa-thers which occupied him for the rest of his life. Jerome, in nine folio volumes, appeared in 1515, Cyprian in 1520, Ambrose in 1527, and Augustine in 1529. These were frequently revised and were accom-panied by smaller undertakings.

It would be a mistake to conclude, however, that Erasmus resolved the conflict between piety and learning by becoming a biblical editor. His interests and methods were not altogether those of a modern scientific scholar, and he was never the dry-as-dust type. "Erasmus' was not the temper of a scholar as we understand it today," observes Allen. "Not for him was the slow labour of digging foundations and laying brick to brick to build up an edifice. His work was always done in heat, under the passion of his demand for knowledge. He read, he wrote,

[14] Allen, Ep. 149; Nichols, Ep. 143.
[15] Allen, Ep. 182; Nichols, Ep. 182.

'tumultuarie,' 'praecipitanter.' When he had formed a design, he liked
to carry it out 'uno impetu.' " [16] Equally significant is the fact that he
never went so far as to regard a knowledge of classical literature and
rhetoric as simply an instrument for the establishment and prepara-
tion of the text of the Scriptures. Despite his assertions that he has
outgrown his early naive delight in mere matters of style and that he
longs to be at work on the New Testament and to throw aside all
worldly tasks, he continued to value, or at least to enjoy, rhetorical
skill and the content of the pagan classics for their own sakes. This is
evident in the *Adagia,* in his translations from the Greek, especially
Lucian, and in the theoretical description of a proper secondary school
curriculum which he prepared for Colet. The latter, entitled *De Ratione Studii,* was begun perhaps as early as 1497, and was first published without authorization in 1511 from a manuscript that Erasmus
had apparently completed while in Italy in 1508. He was doubtless planning its revision and enlargement in the following year, at the same
time that he was writing *The Praise of Folly.* It describes, presumably,
the kind of education that Erasmus had desired in his own youth and
which he had been obliged to acquire through private study. It was
introduced into practice at Colet's new school, St. Paul's, and became
"the fundamental philosophy of the grammar school in England." [17]
It is chiefly concerned, as Erasmus explains at the beginning, with
"the knowledge of words" rather than with "the knowledge of truths,"
for "if the latter is first in importance the former is acquired first in
order of time." The student was to be thoroughly grounded, largely
by inductive methods, in Greek and Latin grammar, in the technique
of reading analytically for both content and style, and in composition
and declamation. As he read, the student was to "pick out any unusual
word, archaism, or innovation, anything reasoned or invented unusu-
ally well, or aptly turned, any outstanding ornament of speech, any
adage, exemplum, *sententia.* . . ." [18] He should have at the tip of his
"tongue a *summa* of rhetoric; that is, propositions, the 'places' of
proofs, exornations, amplifications, formulas of transitions." [19] To aid
the student, Erasmus had written two textbooks, *Copia* and *Parabolae,*
which showed how to develop and amplify a theme by means of logical analysis, examples, figures of speech, and exornation or the "gor-
gious beautifying of the tongue with borowed wordes, and change of
sentence or speech with much varietie." [20] At the climax of the course

[16] "Erasmus' Services to Learning," p. 366.

[17] T. W. Baldwin, *William Shakespere's Small Latine & Lesse Greeke* (University
of Illinois Press, 1944), I, 94. *De Ratione Studii* is elaborately analyzed by Baldwin,
and is abbreviated and paraphrased by W. H. Woodward in *Desiderius Erasmus
Concerning the Aims and Methods of Education,* Cambridge, 1904.

[18] Baldwin, I, 83.

[19] *Ibid.,* I, 81.

[20] *Ibid.,* I, 82. Quoted from Wilson's *The Art of Rhetorique.*

came the formal declamation, which the student studied part by part, "from exordium to narration, from narration to division, from division to reasoning, from proposition to proposition, from reason to reason, from the argument to the epilogue or peroration." [21] The student developed facility by treating the same subject in a variety of ways, by essaying the "suasory, dissuasory, hortatory, dehortatory, narrative, gratulatory, expostulatory, commendatory, consolatory." He would be asked "to vituperate Julius Caesar, or praise Socrates in the demonstrative type." [22] Although the assigned readings were obviously meant to "improve" the student and were therefore somewhat moralistic, Baldwin is probably right in concluding "that Erasmus had a genuine literary interest, and that he thought these works should be taught first as literature, only secondly as morality, even though the works should be selected and taught so that morality would not suffer." [23] "Indeed we may say," Erasmus asserts strongly, "that a genuine student ought to grasp the meaning and force of every fact or idea that he meets with in his reading, otherwise their treatment through epithet, metaphor, or simile will be to him obscure and confused." [24] It is clear that Erasmus had a lively interest in stylistic techniques and devices, and in fact the training which he advocates in such matters may seem excessively thorough, but sentences like the one that has just been quoted suggest that he understood the organic relationship of style and content.

This impression is supported by the course of his translations from the Greek. His immediate purpose was to increase his knowledge of the language; he also provided himself with the literary gifts that were required under the system of patronage that then prevailed. His first translation was a declamation by the Greek sophist, Libanius, the subject of which was Menelaus demanding of the Trojans the restoration of Helen. "The whole thing is of little importance," he wrote in 1503;[25] nor did he have a much higher regard for his versions of Euripides' *Hecuba* and *Iphigenia*. He had selected the plays because of their rhetoric rather than because of their poetic power. Euripides is interesting, he wrote in 1507, for "the closeness of his arguments and a sort of declamatory power of persuading and dissuading. . . ." [26] Not until he translated Lucian did Erasmus become, in his own words, "a genuine student" of Greek. Thirty-two of the dialogues were translated into Latin by Sir Thomas More and Erasmus and published at Paris in 1506. Twenty-eight of them were by Erasmus.[27]

[21] *Ibid.*, I, 89.
[22] *Ibid.*, I, 88.
[23] *Ibid.*, I, 99.
[24] *Ibid.*, I, 85.
[25] Allen, Ep. 177; Nichols, Ep. 173.
[26] Allen, Ep. 208; Nichols, Ep. 205.
[27] Craig Thompson, *The Translations of Lucian by Erasmus and St. Thomas More*, Ithaca, N. Y., 1940.

III

We began this brief interview of Erasmus' intellectual development with the aim of suggesting the growing complexity of his mind and his consequent need for a correspondingly complex mode of expression. His various interests and attitudes appear to form a number of paradoxes. He was a man of great energy, often impulsive and passionate, who participated intensely in a considerable variety of experiences; yet he was thoroughly critical of the world in which he lived so vigorously. His own description of Sir Thomas More in the Preface to *The Praise of Folly* comes to mind: "In this mortal life you are a kind of Democritus. You have the rare wisdom needed to oppose the crowd, and at the same time you enjoy getting along with all men on all occasions." He had a warm sympathy for confused and erring men, but few human hypocrisies and pretensions escaped his censure. He devoted himself to classical and biblical learning with immense and fruitful energy; yet he was altogether scornful of most of the scholars of his day, and even questioned the validity of humane knowledge as contrasted with natural instincts and Christian simplicity. It is clear, in short, that Erasmus needed a many-sided symbol through which to express himself. He found it in the figure of folly or the fool, which was at hand in both life and literature.

The Ship of Fools, in its various forms, was the best known literary treatment of folly. Erasmus knew *Stultifera Navis* (1497), the Latin translation of Sebastian Brant's *Narrenschiff* (1494); he may have been acquainted with the other Latin and French enlargements; and while he was writing *The Praise of Folly,* two English versions appeared, the best being Alexander Barclay's *The Ship of Fools of the World.* Some of the same excesses and hypocrisies are quite naturally satirized in both *The Praise of Folly* and *The Ship of Fools,* but the basic aims are different. *The Ship of Fools* is essentially moralistic and conservative. It is a collection of pictorially illustrated aphorisms designed primarily to enforce conventional behavior. A fool is anyone who does not conform to the established order. Prudence and industry are chiefly commended; and it is even implied that a sensible life on earth is the surest road to heaven. Brant and Barclay "projected no better picture of life on earth and no fuller vision of heaven than that given by a sincere, pedestrian, static comprehension of feudal and Catholic teaching." [28]

Erasmus added far more to the symbol of folly than he may have received from Brant. By having Folly speak, Erasmus was able to in-

---

[28] Barbara Swain, *Fools and Folly during the Middle Ages and the Renaissance* (New York, 1932), pp. 132–133.

dulge his skill in the composition of the formal oration, and at the same time to remind his readers through parody, that it and other rhetorical modes should never be more than means to an end. Folly, likewise, could very easily be made to present the most telling of arguments for the natural and instinctive life; in the same breath she could be used to imply that such a life is foolish indeed, an unfortunate relaxation from the disciplined and examined existence which man is potentially capable of achieving. At the end, she could be sublimated into the Christian fool and in this form affirm for Erasmus the ultimate values of Christian humanism.

It has often been suggested that Erasmus learned much of his satiric subtlety and his skill in the manipulation of the symbol of folly from Lucian. We have seen that by 1506 he had become a thorough Lucianist, and that fact is clearly reflected in *The Praise of Folly.* "The early part," as Hudson notices, "is Lucianic in its scoffing at the gods of mythology; and further on Erasmus borrows from Lucian the view of the world as seen from heaven or from a great height, the world compared to a stage, and other devices." Hudson goes on to compare the irony of the two writers: "It is less obviously benevolent than Socratic irony. It is likely to hold itself, as well as other things, lightly. It cuts more than one way." He defines one Lucianic device, learned parody, and observes that "We find this device in Erasmus, of course. Early in the eulogy he begins sprinkling in Greek words and phrases, and continues doing so to the end. But also early in it he singles out as one of the bad habits of modern rhetoricians this sprinkling of Greek words and phrases in their Latin compositions; he admits that he copies them. They do so, he says, to show that they are bilingual—a distinction shared by the horse-leech. They also seek to confuse and overawe their readers. Then he goes on with the practice." [29]

Although the Lucianic element in Erasmus is certainly extensive and significant, there is an important difference between the two writers. The nature of that difference can be suggested by comparing their use of the device of viewing the world as a stage seen from a great height. Lucian's version appears in the dialogue *Menippus or Necromantia,* in which Menippus seeks a definition of the good life from the wise Teiresias in the underworld. There he finds that death has levelled all worldly distinctions; "for none of their former means of identification abode with them, but their bones were all alike, undefined, unlabelled, and unable ever again to be distinguished by anyone." Then follows the passage in question:

> So as I [Menippus] looked at them [the dead] it seemed to me that human life is like a long pageant, and that all its trappings are supplied

[29] Hoyt Hudson, *The Praise of Folly* (Princeton University Press, 1941), p. xix.

and distributed by Fortune, who arrays the participants in various costumes of many colours. Taking one person, it may be, she attires him
royally, placing a tiarra upon his head, giving him body-guards, and
encircling his brow with the diadem; but upon another she puts the
costume of a slave. Again, she makes up one person so that he is handsome,
but causes another to be ugly and ridiculous. I suppose that the show
must needs be diversified. And often, in the very middle of the pageant,
she exchanges the costumes of several players; instead of allowing them
to finish the pageant in the parts that had been assigned to them, she
reapparels them, forcing Croesus to assume the dress of a slave and a
captive, and shifting Maeandrius, who formerly paraded among the servants, into the imperial habit of Polycrates. For a brief space she lets
them use their costumes, but when the time of the pageant is over, each
gives back the properties and lays off the costume along with his body,
becoming what he was before birth, no different from his neighbor. Some,
however, are so ungrateful that when Fortune appears to them and asks
her trappings back, they are vexed and indignant, as if they were being
robbed of their own property, instead of giving back what they had
borrowed for a little time.

I suppose you have often seen these stage-folk who act in tragedies,
and according to the demands of the play become at one moment Creons,
and again Priams and Agammemnons; the very one, it may be, who a
short time ago assumed with great dignity the part of Cecrops, or of
Erectheus soon appears as a servant at the bidding of the poet. And when
at length the play comes to an end, each of them strips off his gold-be-
spangled robe, lays aside his mask, steps out of his buskins, and goes about
in poverty and humility. . . . That is what human affairs are like, it
seemed to me as I looked.[30]

The passage is a clear example of dramatic irony, in which the
spectator's superior insight enables him to see that the actor is ignorant
and is doomed to fail. A wise man, in short, can do nothing more
than laugh at life and attempt to safeguard himself by leading a simple existence that change will but slightly disorder. Lucian begins the
dialogue with the aim of exposing the arrogant pretensions of hair-
splitting philosophers and rich men of affairs; he ends by shrugging
his shoulders at all human efforts. The debunking is so thorough that
there is no positive ground left to stand on.

The comparable passage in *The Praise of Folly*[31] opens with Folly
praising herself paradoxically for prudence or worldly wisdom, which,
she argues, is learned only from experience. Since the wise man (of
the Lucianic type) deliberately avoids experience, he can never become
truly prudent. Of course he defends his behavior by asserting that
worldly values are wrong, but this is a patent rationalizing of his own
weakness. False modesty and fear, says Folly, prevent him from being

[30] Tr. A. M. Harmon, Loeb Classical Library, IV, 99–101.
[31] See below, pp. 64–66.

a successful man of action; and then in order to preserve his ego, he makes a virtue of those very inhibitions. If they were removed, Folly remarks, "there is no telling how far one might go."

The satiric ambiguity of that statement concludes one point of view and introduces another. Grant that the real reason for some so-called wise men's choice of the life of simplicity and retirement is that they are deficient in animal energy and active ability, still it will be argued that we should "prefer the kind of prudence which consists in clear understanding." "Very well," answers Folly, "then let me tell you how far those who boast of having that quality really are from it." What follows is a description of the only way of life logically open to the man of "clear understanding" and an assessment of its cost. He will know, of course, that worldly values are the opposite of the true ones. "All human affairs, like the Sileni of Alcibiades, have two opposite aspects." What is commonly regarded as beautiful is really ugly; a king, who is thought to be rich and powerful, is actually the poorest of men if he lacks the goods of the spirit, and so on. It is evident, then, that the man of "clear understanding" must see life as a "kind of stage play through which men pass in various disguises." He may either retire, as Lucian suggests, and laugh at the comedy, "taking nothing seriously"; or he may act affirmatively by unmasking the actors. But to "destroy the illusion" created by the masks and costumes "is to upset the whole play," and it "is performed in no other way." "The masks and costumes are precisely what hold the eyes of the spectators." If a man speaks out against the unexamined life, what will he "gain by it except to be regarded as dangerously insane by everyone?" This kind of Socratic prudence or wisdom is obviously anti-social and impracticable. Therefore, concludes Folly smugly, "true prudence . . . consists in not desiring more wisdom than is proper to mortals"; and if anyone still argues that conformity to the ways of the world "is folly itself," she will not deny it; "yet they must in turn admit that it is also to act the play of life."

From even this short summary, it is clear that Erasmus' version of the metaphor of life as a stage play is more complex than Lucian's. Lucianic irony rarely exceeds the limits set for that device by the classical rhetoricians. They discuss irony briefly as a forensic weapon and as an urbane kind of jesting; it is useful in satire or in the vituperative portrait, and its restraint and subtlety recommend it to the gentleman wit.[32] Erasmian irony, on the other hand, produces a meaning comparable to that derived from a play or from any piece of literature conceived as drama. The irony is composed of the simultaneous ex-

[32] See *Rhetorica ad Alexandrum, Works of Aristotle,* ed. W. D. Ross (Oxford, 1924), XI, 1441b; Cicero, *De oratore,* II, 66–67; and Quintilian, *Institutio oratoria,* VI, 2, 3, 54, IX, 1, 2.

pression of several points of view, just as a play is composed of speeches by many different characters; and the meaning of the irony and of the play is not that of any one point of view or of any one character, but of all of them interacting upon each other. The result is not paralysis or abject relativism, but a larger truth than that presented by any one of the elements alone.[33]

Folly argues that in a world of fools it is indeed folly to be wise, and we may be momentarily won over by her good-natured energy and her keen insight into the real motives of her professed enemies. As the dramatic argument proceeds, however, we begin to have doubts; other points of view are presented and Folly herself degenerates. She becomes arrogant and then careless. After all, as she asserts, the play of life is put on in no other way but hers; all men, including her opponents, are fools; and since everyone is really on her side all the time, the notion that an argument is in progress or is even possible is a preposterous fiction. Finally, she gives up that fiction entirely. Very well, she concludes, my program is folly, but that's life and the only possible life, so nothing can be done about it. In the meantime, however, other voices in the irony have been explaining precisely what can be done about it. Their program is nothing less than the radical one proposed by Christ and Socrates; and when Folly's energy and shrewdness degenerate into complacent apathy and cynicism, the positive force is transferred to the new point of view, which now attracts us as Folly had at the beginning. The final or total meaning is not expressed by either point of view exclusively, just as the meaning of a play is not expressed by any one character alone.

By writing ironically, Erasmus is able to avoid the narrow and unrealistic dogmatism of the Sunday sermon and of the devil's cynicism. He advocates no "cloistered virtue," nor does he assert that the world will be suddenly reformed. He admits the presence of folly within us, he recognizes its natural energy and peculiar honesty, and at the same time he reveals its radical limitations. Like Milton, he is not explaining anything away; he is rather reasserting and revitalizing the humanistic conception of what it means to be a man. We are not allowed to shy away into Lucianic indifference, into comfortable conformity with folly, or into the idealistic illusion that folly does not exist or that it will soon be dissipated. The irony of Erasmus obliges us to look squarely and justly at the human spectacle.

IV

Closer to the essential spirit of *The Praise of Folly* than *The Ship of Fools* or even than Lucian's dialogues, is the first book of More's

[33] See I. A. Richards, *Principles of Literacy Criticism* (New York, 1924), pp. 246 ff., and Kenneth Burke, "Four Master Tropes," *Kenyon Review*, Autumn, 1941, pp. 432–435.

Utopia. Although it was composed seven years after Erasmus had finished his eulogy, it reflects an interest of long-standing, and it is concerned with topics that More and Erasmus must have often discussed. The tone of More's dedicatory epistle to Peter Giles, an old friend of Erasmus, is as subtly dramatic as anything in *The Praise of Folly.* More poses as a rather fussy little scholar. He is worried about the exact length of the bridge of Amaurote; and still worse, he has absent-mindedly forgotten to ask the whereabouts of Utopia. He wonders, too, whether the book should even be published, and whether it is really wise to labor for knowledge rather than to lead a life of easy pleasure. He observes that the general public judge that "they which lead a merry and jocund life . . . may seem to be in a much better state or case, than they that vex and unquiet themselves with cares and study. . . ." [34] That recalls *The Praise of Folly,* as does More's satiric description of the readers who may receive his book unfavorably. Some scorn all learning; others, whose little learning has made them pedantic, reject "whatsoever is not stuffed full of old moth-eaten terms." Some are so sour that they permit no mirth or sport, and still others are afraid of anything satiric. Then, too, there are those who "sit upon their ale-benches, and there among their cups they give judgment of the wits of writers. . . ." [35]

The first book itself opens with the well known fiction of the conversation between Giles, More, and Hythloday, who has just returned from the New World. He is urged to serve the public by offering the fruits of his learning and remarkable experience to some monarch; but he reminds his two friends that proposals like his would be ill received by kings and courtiers, who are more interested in military conquest and feats of chivalry than in good government. They would resent his suggestions as constituting an attack on their very wisdom. If every other defense failed them, then they would argue that established customs "pleased our forefathers and ancestors; would God we could be so wise as they were: and as though they had wittily concluded the matter, and with this answer stopped every man's mouth, they sit down again. As who should say, it were a very dangerous matter, if a man in any point should be found wiser than his forefathers were." [36] The basic problem here is precisely the same as that in *The Praise of Folly.* How can rational and Christian advice be presented persuasively to a worldly government? How can wisdom become effective in a world of folly and be united with the energy of successful men of action? How can the costly gap between the ideal and the actual be closed? What action is available to the Christian humanist?

Hythloday remarks drily that he has often been rebuffed by com-

[34] *Utopia,* ed. J. R. Lumby (Cambridge, 1897), p. 14.
[35] *Ibid.,* p. 15.
[36] *Ibid.,* p. 26.

placent and arrogant men of affairs, and even once in England. The
occasion was a dinner at the home of Cardinal Morton, More's old
patron; and Hythloday's opponent was a reactionary lawyer. In the
course of the conversation Hythloday analyzed the major social abuses
in England and suggested humane and reasonable remedies for them;
but the lawyer objected that such remedies would undermine the English way of life. "And as he was thus saying, he shaked his head, and
made a wry mouth, and so he held his peace. And all that were there
present, with one assent agreed to his saying." [37] From this experience,
concludes Hythloday, one "may right well perceive how little the courtiers would regard and esteem me and my sayings." [38] When More
persists in his urging, Hythloday uses another example. "Well, suppose
I were with the French king," he begins, "when he was discussing with
his craftiest advisers how to enlarge his power and domain; and suppose that I, simple fool, should suggest that his real business was to
rule France well; how do you think my advice would be received?"
Not very thankfully, admits More; still, this is "school philosophy,"
not unpleasant among friends, "but in the councils of the kings, where
greater matters be debated and reasoned with great authority, these
things have no place." [39] That is exactly what I have been saying,
answers Hythloday. No, continues More, what is needed here is a
more civil kind of philosophy; and to make his point clear, More, like
Erasmus, uses the metaphor of the stage play.

> If you should suddenly come upon the stage in a philosopher's ap-
> parel . . . , you must needs mar and pervert the play that is in hand,
> though the stuff that you bring be much better. What part soever you
> have taken upon you, play that as well as you can and make the best
> of it. . . . If evil opinions . . . can not be utterly and quite plucked out
> of their hearts . . . ; yet for this cause you must not leave and forsake
> the commonwealth. . . . But you must with a crafty wile and a subtle
> train study and endeavor yourself, as much as in you lies, to handle the
> matter wittily and handsomely for the purpose, and that which you can
> not turn to good, so to order it that it will not be very bad. [40]

Hythloday answers that to tamper with the means is to aim at
another end and to miss the one desired. If he enters the play of life
and conforms to the folly of the world, he will be as foolish as the rest:
"while that I go about to remedy the madness of others, I should be
even as mad as they." [41] To prove his point, Hythloday cites the example of the preachers, who have lowered the ideals of Christ in order
to meet the world on its own level. "Whereby I can not see what

[37] *Ibid.*, p. 44.
[38] *Ibid.*, p. 48.
[39] *Ibid.*, p. 57.
[40] *Ibid.*, pp. 58–59.
[41] *Ibid.*, p. 59.

good they have done; but that men may more safely and easily be evil." [42] Liberal legislation and other half-way measures, he continues, may ease conditions, but will never cure them. Only an equal distribution of property will ever do that. To this radical remedy, More presents two conventional objections. First, communism destroys initiative and leads to lawlessness; and second, our own way of doing things is older and better than any newfangled system. "I marvel not," answers Hythloday in conclusion, "that you be of this opinion. For you conceive in your mind either none at all, or else a very false image and similitude of this thing." [43] When the ideal, or Utopia, is clearly conceived, the conventional objections fall aside. In Utopia, initiative and order arise from devotion to the general welfare, and they are therefore superior to the kind produced by profits and legal restrictions. Furthermore, the merit of a government is not to be judged by its age, but by its receptiveness to new and worthwhile ideas; and in this respect the Utopians are preeminent. And so Hythloday proceeds to a description of his ideal commonwealth, yet not without acknowledging once more that it will be a long time indeed before Utopia is achieved in a world of folly.

The striking thing here, as in *The Praise of Folly*, is that the final effect is not cynical, even though Hythloday can see no immediate solution to the problem. It is not suggested that men should abandon their ideals because they can not be fully actualized. It is implied, rather, that a necessary step in bringing the ideal and the actual closer together is a sharper definition of both. The great obstacles are a failure to see things as they actually are, and a failure to conceive the ideal in its most severely logical form. The followers of Folly are blinded by custom and sentimentality.

In *The Praise of Folly* the ideal, which is indirectly affirmed throughout the book, is openly carried to its logical conclusion in the description of the Christian fool. The section is begun with characteristic lightness and indirection as a parody on the irresponsible citation of authorities by lawyers and theologians. After playing fast and loose with a series of biblical passages containing the word *fool*, Folly gradually becomes more and more serious as she first gives an example of legitimate scriptural interpretation, and then sharpens and sublimates the meaning of folly to the wisdom that passes human prudence and understanding. "Let him that seems to be wise among you become a fool, that he may be wise." [44] She goes on to state that "The Christian religion on the whole seems to have some kinship with folly, while it has none at all with wisdom." The first proof is the ironic observation that children, old people, women, and fools "are ever nearest

[42] *Ibid.*, p. 60.
[43] *Ibid.*, p. 64.
[44] See pp. 123–124.

the altars, led no doubt solely by instinct." But this is fooling, or
definition by indirection, for these are no more true Christian fools
than are those "founders of religion" who "have been the bitterest
foes of learning." The real Christian fools are those who have been
so possessed with piety that they have died to the world in order to
gain life. Their lot is like that of the man who left Plato's cave and
saw reality, and their folly is like the madness of Plato's lover who
lost himself in the object of his adoration. This sublimation of folly
is the ideal expressed in its severest form; and when all the sentimental
evasions are finally dispensed with, the effect is not cynicism but rather
that paradoxical exhilaration produced by tragedy.

V

The other quality which safeguards both *The Praise of Folly* and
The Utopia from cynicism is harder to suggest by means of analysis.
Hudson is trying to define it when he remarks: "Yet something is still
left over . . . —principally the gusto, abandon, and joyous release
which supply so much of the book's appeal, and perhaps a great part
of its real message." [45] Miss Swain is pointing at this quality when she
observes that

> neither Brant nor Barclay really transported their readers beyond
> wisdom's knee into the carnival pageant of obstreperous and irresponsible
> life [as Erasmus did]. [His Folly evokes] . . . the gay confidence in vitality
> which lends a keener edge to criticism of conduct. . . . By virtue of his
> faith in man he united the old feeling of mystery and freedom connected
> with the wanton folk fool to his picture of erring fools in society; he
> censured earthly morality in the double name of earthly and spiritual
> vitality.[46]

This quality of energy works throughout *The Praise of Folly* against
the cynical flippancy and irresponsibility that Hudson rightly calls the
typical perversion of irony. Erasmus affirms its presence in mankind in
two oblique and related ways; it appears as the uninhibited force of
natural instincts, and as the immense effort with which man struggles
to achieve his ends, valueless though they may be. Folly, first of all,
is a name for all that is natural and fecund. She was conceived in
passion and born out of wedlock. Her parents were Youth, the gayest
of the nymphs, and Plutus, the young and intoxicated king of the gods.
Her birthplace was the Fortunate Isles, where there is no labor and
where all things thrive naturally. She alone presides over the conception of life. Even Jove must play the fool when he is engaged, as he

[45] Hudson, *op. cit.*, p. xxxiii.
[46] Swain, *op. cit.*, pp. 136, 139.

always is, in begetting children; and the solemn stoic must remove his beard and unbend when he wishes to become a father. We catch the note of subversive and energetic delight in Folly's account of conception, during which the most rational and pompous beings are reduced willy-nilly to fellowship with the lowliest creatures. Her reminder that even the most dignified of men are conceived and born in this ludicrous fashion is true ironic comedy. She exposes the limitations of all highly respectable forms of behavior. They are advertised as the only forms through which man can truly express himself, but Folly reveals that they express only a fraction of the potential energy and value in life. She reminds us that when people grow up and succumb to the conventions of adulthood, they suffer a loss of youthful energy and flexibility. To aim at the stoic ideal of god-like rationalism is really to become a sort of marble monster. Nothing escapes such a creature, observes Folly sarcastically; he evaluates everything rigidly, and he excuses nothing. Folly tells him to be himself, to be natural. She pictures him in all his ridiculous pride, and the comic sight reminds us that his vaunted self-control is an unwarranted separation of reason and emotion. Let him be natural and foolish so that he may be truly wise.

Folly, in the second place, is a name for all misdirected effort, for all of man's elaborate pains to gain the wrong thing. There are the flabby-breasted old women, painted, plucked and corsetted, who valiantly chase men and their own lost youth from bar to bar. There are the descendents of the Best Families, as senseless as the busts of their ancestors, whose titles they know by heart. These and other earnest fools put on a superb daily performance for the gods, who leave the office early to watch the show from the grandstand. Here is a man who carefully manages to marry a dowry instead of a woman. Over there is a person who is properly stricken with grief. He has made elaborate funeral arrangements and has hired mourners as if they were so many actors. He could squeeze out a tear at the grave of his mother-in-law. Here are respectable business men, lying, cheating, swindling, and misleading the public in order to make money that their heirs will spend. And all these fools happily applaud themselves. After all, "What is more courteous than the way two mules scratch each other?" The most devoted and self-sacrificing followers of Folly, however, are the scholars, "a tormented, calamity-ridden, God-forsaken body of men." This distinguished student of linguistics, after twenty years of research, has conclusively defined the eight parts of speech, a thing that the Greeks and Romans were somehow unable to do; and he becomes fighting mad if anyone calls one of his conjunctions an adverb. When the scholars discover the name of an author's second cousin in some moldy manuscript there is no end to the exulting and congratulating. If one of them makes the slightest scholarly slip, however, he is sternly and publicly reprimanded. At the same time, they are very generous with their predecessors. If they encounter something in the writings of the Apostles that is not properly documented or foot-noted, they excuse it on the grounds that it would be unfair to demand the methods of modern scholarship from men who never went to a graduate school and obtained a doctor's degree. They form cliques and invent controversies in order to give the impression that they are threshing out major issues. The members of the same clique applaud each other and express horror at the dangerously unsound critical principles of their so-called opponents. All of this immense and mis-guided effort is certainly folly, yet it is also indirect evidence of man's power for achievement. Erasmus derides the preoccupation with ap-pearances, but by arguing as Folly he at the same time affirms the energy in life and the possibility of expressing it through wiser modes of action.

One can understand why some parts of *The Praise of Folly* might be called ancient journalism. Alchemists, courtiers, and theologians may have their modern counterparts, yet they are indeed extinct as Erasmus knew them. Nevertheless, a book that deals with the role of the intellectual in practical affairs or with the problem of reconciling dictatorial efficiency and humane reflection, to name only two major themes, is scarcely outmoded. Nor can Erasmian irony be called cow-ardice when it is seen to criticize in order to affirm what is ideal. We may not become fools for Christ's sake, but the infectious exu-berance of Folly takes us out of our conventional selves and gives us sight of what we might become. When it is carefully read, *The Praise of Folly* is a lively and valuable commentary on our own times.

The Comedy of Life

by Johann Huizinga

While he rode over the mountain passes,[1] Erasmus's restless spirit, now unfettered for some days by set tasks, occupied itself with everything he had studied and read in the last few years, and with everything he had seen. What ambition, what self-deception, what pride and conceit filled the world! He thought of Thomas More, whom he was now to see again—that most witty and wise of all his friends, with that curious name *Moros*, the Greek word for a fool, which so ill became his personality. Anticipating the gay jests which More's conversation promised, there grew in his mind that masterpiece of humour and wise irony, *Moriae Encomium*, the *Praise of Folly*. The world as the scene of universal folly; folly as the indispensable element making life and society possible and all this put into the mouth of Stultitia —Folly—itself (true antitype of Minerva), who in a panegyric on her own power and usefulness, praises herself. As to form it is a *Declamatio*, such as he had translated from the Greek of Libanius. As to the spirit, a revival of Lucian, whose *Gallus*, translated by him three years before, may have suggested the theme. It must have been in the incomparably lucid moments of that brilliant intellect. All the particulars of classic reading which the year before he worked up in the new edition of the *Adagia* were still at his immediate disposal in that retentive and capacious memory. Reflecting at his ease on all that wisdom of the ancients, he secreted the juices required for his expostulation.

He arrived in London, took up his abode in More's house in Bucklersbury, and there, tortured by nephritic pains, he wrote down in a few days, without having his books with him, the perfect work of art that must have been ready in his mind. Stultitia was truly born in the manner of her serious sister Pallas.

---

[1] That he conceived the work in the Alps follows from the fact that he tells us explicitly that it happened while riding, whereas, after passing through Switzerland, he travelled by boat. A. 1, IV 216.62.

As to form and imagery the *Moria* is faultless, the product of the inspired moments of creative impulse. The figure of an orator confronting her public is sustained to the last in a masterly way. We see the faces of the auditors light up with glee when Folly appears in the pulpit; we hear the applause interrupting her words. There is a wealth of fancy, coupled with so much soberness of line and colour, such reserve, that the whole presents a perfect instance of that harmony which is the essence of Renaissance expression. There is no exuberance, in spite of the multiplicity of matter and thought, but a temperateness, a smoothness, an airiness and clearness which are as gladdening as they are relaxing. In order perfectly to realize the artistic perfection of Erasmus's book we should compare it with Rabelais.

"Without me," says Folly, "the world cannot exist for a moment. For is not all that is done at all among mortals, full of folly; is it not performed by fools and for fools?" "No society, no cohabitation can be pleasant or lasting without folly; so much so, that a people could not stand its prince, nor the master his man, nor the maid her mistress, nor the tutor his pupil, nor the friend his friend, nor the wife her husband for a moment longer, if they did not now and then err together, now flatter each other; now sensibly conniving at things, now smearing themselves with some honey of folly." In that sentence the summary of the *Laus* is contained. Folly here is worldly wisdom, resignation and lenient judgement.

He who pulls off the masks in the comedy of life is ejected. What is the whole life of mortals but a sort of play in which each actor appears on the boards in his specific mask and acts his part till the stage-manager calls him off? He acts wrongly who does not adapt himself to existing conditions, and demands that the game shall be a game no longer. It is the part of the truly sensible to mix with all people, either conniving readily at their folly, or affably erring like themselves.

And the necessary driving power of all human action is "Philautia," Folly's own sister: self-love. He who does not please himself effects little. Take away that condiment of life and the word of the orator cools, the poet is laughed at, the artist perishes with his art.

Folly in the garb of pride, of vanity, of vainglory, is the hidden spring of all that is considered high and great in this world. The state with its posts of honour, patriotism and national pride; the stateliness of ceremonies, the delusion of caste and nobility—what is it but folly? War, the most foolish thing of all, is the origin of all heroism. What prompted the Deciuses, what Curtius, to sacrifice themselves? Vainglory. It is this folly which produces states; through her, empires, religion, law-courts, exist.

This is bolder and more chilling than Machiavelli, more detached than Montaigne. But Erasmus will not have it credited to him: it is

Folly who speaks. He purposely makes us tread the round of the *circulus vitiosus*, as in the old saw: A Cretan said, all Cretans are liars.

Wisdom is to folly as reason is to passion. And there is much more passion than reason in the world. That which keeps the world going, the fount of life, is folly. For what else is love? Why do people marry, if not out of folly, which sees no objections? All enjoyment and amusement is only a condiment of folly. When a wise man wishes to become a father, he has first to play the fool. For what is more foolish than the game of procreation?

Unperceived the orator has incorporated here with folly all that is vitality and the courage of life. Folly is spontaneous energy that no one can do without. He who is perfectly sensible and serious cannot live. The more people get away from me, Stultitia, the less they live. Why do we kiss and cuddle little children, if not because they are still so delightfully foolish. And what else makes youth so elegant?

Now look at the truly serious and sensible. They are awkward at everything, at meal-time, at a dance, in playing, in social intercourse. If they have to buy, or to contract, things are sure to go wrong. Quintilian says that stage fright bespeaks the intelligent orator, who knows his faults. Right! But does not, then, Quintilian confess openly that wisdom is an impediment to good execution? And has not Stultitia the right to claim prudence for herself, if the wise, out of shame, out of bashfulness, undertake nothing in circumstances where fools pluckily set to work?

Here Erasmus goes to the root of the matter in a psychological sense. Indeed the consciousness of falling short in achievement is the brake clogging action, is the great inertia retarding the progress of the world. Did he know himself for one who is awkward when not bending over his books, but confronting men and affairs?

Folly is gaiety and lightheartedness, indispensable to happiness. The man of mere reason without passion is a stone image, blunt and without any human feeling, a spectre or monster, from whom all fly, deaf to all natural emotions, susceptible neither to love nor compassion. Nothing escapes him, in nothing he errs; he sees through everything, he weighs everything accurately, he forgives nothing, he is only satisfied with himself; he alone is healthy; he alone is king, he alone is free. It is the hideous figure of the doctrinaire which Erasmus is thinking of. Which state, he exclaims, would desire such an absolutely wise man for a magistrate?

He who devotes himself to tasting all the bitterness of life with wise insight would forthwith deprive himself of life. Only folly is a remedy: to err, to be mistaken, to be ignorant is to be human. How much better it is in marriage to be blind to a wife's shortcomings than to make away with oneself out of jealousy and to fill the world with tragedy! Adulation is virtue. There is no cordial devotion without a little adulation. It is the soul of eloquence, of medicine and poetry; it is the honey and the sweetness of all human customs.

Again a series of valuable social qualities is slyly incorporated with folly: benevolence, kindness, inclination to approve and to admire.

But especially to approve of oneself. There is no pleasing others without beginning by flattering ourselves a little and approving of ourselves. What would the world be if everyone was not proud of his standing, his calling, so that no person would change places with another in point of good appearance, of fancy, of good family, of landed property?

Humbug is the right thing. Why should any one desire true erudition? The more incompetent a man, the pleasanter his life is and the more he is admired. Look at professors, poets, orators. Man's mind is so made that he is more impressed by lies than by the truth. Go to church: if the priest deals with serious subjects the whole congregation is dozing, yawning, feeling bored. But when he begins to tell some cock-and-bull story, they awake, sit up, and hang on his lips.

To be deceived, philosophers say, is a misfortune, but not to be deceived is a superlative misfortune. If it is human to err, why should a man be called unhappy because he errs, since he was so born and made, and it is the fate of all? Do we pity a man because he cannot fly or does not walk on four legs? We might as well call the horse unhappy because it does not learn grammar or eat cakes. No creature is unhappy, if it lives according to its nature. The sciences were invented to our utmost destruction; far from conducing to our happiness, they are even in its way, though for its sake they are supposed to have been invented. By the agency of evil demons they have stolen into human life with the other pests. For did not the simple-minded people of the Golden Age live happily, unprovided with any science, only led by nature and instinct? What did they want grammar for, when all spoke the same language? Why have dialectics, when there were no quarrels and no differences of opinion? Why jurisprudence, when there were no bad morals from which good laws sprang? They were too religious to investigate with impious curiosity the secrets of nature, the size, motions, influence of the stars, the hidden cause of things.

It is the old idea, which germinated in antiquity, here lightly touched upon by Erasmus, afterwards proclaimed by Rousseau in bitter earnest: civilization is a plague.

Wisdom is misfortune, but self-conceit is happiness. Grammarians, who wield the sceptre of wisdom—schoolmasters, that is—would be the most wretched of all people if I, Folly, did not mitigate the discomforts of their miserable calling by a sort of sweet frenzy. But what holds good of schoolmasters, also holds good of poets, orators, authors. For them, too, all happiness merely consists in vanity and delusion. The lawyers are no better off and after them come the philosophers.

Next there is a numerous procession of clergy: divines, monks, bishops, cardinals, popes, only interrupted by princes and courtiers.

In the chapters[2] which review these offices and callings, satire has shifted its ground a little. Throughout the work two themes are intertwined: that of salutary folly, which is true wisdom, and that of deluded wisdom, which is pure folly. As they are both put into the mouth of Folly, we should have to invert them both to get truth, if Folly . . . were not wisdom. Now it is clear that the first is the principal theme. Erasmus starts from it; and he returns to it. Only in the middle, as he reviews human accomplishments and dignities in their universal foolishness, the second theme predominates and the book becomes an ordinary satire on human folly, of which there are many though few are so delicate. But in the other parts it is something far deeper.

Occasionally the satire runs somewhat off the line, when Stultitia directly censures what Erasmus wishes to censure; for instance, indulgences, silly belief in wonders, selfish worship of the saints; or gamblers whom she, Folly, ought to praise; or the spirit of systematizing and levelling, and the jealousy of the monks.

For contemporary readers the importance of the *Laus Stultitiae* was, to a great extent, in the direct satire. Its lasting value is in those passages where we truly grant that folly is wisdom and the reverse. Erasmus knows the aloofness of the ground of all things: all consistent thinking out of the dogmas of faith leads to absurdity. Only look at the theological quiddities of effete scholasticism. The apostles would not have understood them: in the eyes of latter-day divines they would have been fools. Holy Scripture itself sides with folly. "The foolishness of God is wiser than men," says Saint Paul. "But God hath chosen the foolish things of the world." "It pleased God by the foolishness (of preaching) to save them that believe." Christ loved the simple-minded and the ignorant: children, women, poor fishermen, nay, even such animals as are farthest removed from vulpine cunning: the ass which he wished to ride, the dove, the lamb, the sheep.

Here there is a great deal behind the seemingly light jest: "Christian religion seems in general to have some affinity with a certain sort of folly." Was it not thought the apostles were full of new wine? And did not the judge say: "Paul, thou art beside thyself"? When are we beside ourselves? When the spirit breaks its fetters and tries to escape from its prison and aspires to liberty. That is madness, but it is also other-worldliness and the highest wisdom. True happiness is in selflessness, in the furore of lovers, whom Plato calls happiest of all. The more absolute love is, the greater and more rapturous is the frenzy.

[2] Erasmus did not divide the book into chapters. It was done by an editor as late as 1765.

Heavenly bliss itself is the greatest insanity; truly pious people enjoy its shadow on earth already in their meditations.

Here Stultitia breaks off her discourse, apologizing in a few words in case she may have been too petulant or talkative, and leaves the pulpit. "So farewell, applaud, live happily, and drink, Moria's illustrious initiates."

It was an unrivalled feat of art even in these last chapters neither to lose the light comical touch, nor to lapse into undisguised profanation. It was only feasible by veritable dancing on the tight-rope of sophistry. In the *Moria* Erasmus is all the time hovering on the brink of profound truths. But what a boon it was—still granted to those times— to be able to treat of all this in a vein of pleasantry. For this should be impressed upon our minds: that the *Moriae Encomium* is a true, gay jest. The laugh is more delicate, but no less hearty than Rabelais's. "Valete, plaudite, vivite, bibite." "All common people abound to such a degree, and everywhere, in so many forms of folly that a thousand Democrituses would be insufficient to laugh at them all (and they would require another Democritus to laugh at them)."

How could one take the *Moria* too seriously, when even More's *Utopia,* which is a true companion-piece to it and makes such a grave impression on us, is treated by its author and Erasmus as a mere jest? There is a place where the *Laus* seems to touch both More and Rabelais; the place where Stultitia speaks of her father, Plutus, the god of wealth, at whose beck all things are turned topsy-turvy, according to whose will all human affairs are regulated—war and peace, government and counsel, justice and treaties. He has begotten her on the nymph Youth, not a senile, purblind Plutus, but a fresh god, warm with youth and nectar, like another Gargantua.

The figure of Folly, of gigantic size, looms large in the period of the Renaissance. She wears a fool's cap and bells. People laughed loudly and with unconcern at all that was foolish, without discriminating between species of folly. It is remarkable that even in the *Laus,* delicate as it is, the author does not distinguish between the unwise or the silly, between fools and lunatics. Holbein, illustrating Erasmus, knows but of one representation of a fool: with a staff and ass's ears. Erasmus speaks without clear transition, now of foolish persons and now of real lunatics. They are happiest of all, he makes Stultitia say: they are not frightened by spectres and apparitions; they are not tortured by the fear of impending calamities; everywhere they bring mirth, jests, frolic and laughter. Evidently he here means harmless imbeciles, who, indeed, were often used as jesters. This identification of denseness and insanity is kept up, however, like the confusion of the comic and the simply ridiculous, and all this is well calculated to make us feel how wide the gap has already become that separates us from Erasmus.

In later years he always spoke slightingly of his *Moria*. He considered it so unimportant, he says, as to be unworthy of publication, yet no work of his had been received with such applause. It was a trifle and not at all in keeping with his character. More had made him write it, as if a camel were made to dance. But these disparaging utterances were not without a secondary purpose. The *Moria* had not brought him only success and pleasure. The exceedingly susceptible age in which he lived had taken the satire in very bad part, where it seemed to glance at offices and orders, although in his preface he had tried to safeguard himself from the reproach of irreverence. His airy play with the texts of Holy Scripture had been too venturesome for many. His friend Martin van Dorp upbraided him with having made a mock of eternal life. Erasmus did what he could to convince evil-thinkers that the purpose of the *Moria* was no other than to exhort people to be virtuous. In affirming this he did his work injustice: it was much more than that. But in 1515 he was no longer what he had been in 1509. Repeatedly he had been obliged to defend his most witty work. Had he known that it would offend, he might have kept it back, he writes in 1517 to an acquaintance at Louvain. Even towards the end of his life, he warded off the insinuations of Alberto Pio of Carpi in a lengthy expostulation.

Erasmus made no further ventures in the genre of the *Praise of Folly*. One might consider the treatise *Lingua,* which he published in 1525, as an attempt to make a companionpiece to the *Moria*. The book is called *Of the Use and Abuse of the Tongue*. In the opening pages there is something that reminds us of the style of the *Laus,* but it lacks all the charm both of form and of thought.

Should one pity Erasmus because, of all his publications, collected in ten folio volumes, only the *Praise of Folly* has remained a really popular book? It is, apart from the *Colloquies,* perhaps the only one of his works that is still read for its own sake. The rest is now only studied from a historical point of view, for the sake of becoming acquainted with his person or his times. It seems to me that perfect justice has been done in this case. The *Praise of Folly* is his best work. He wrote other books, more erudite, some more pious—some perhaps of equal or greater influence on his time. But each has had its day. *Moriae Encomium* alone was to be immortal. For only when humour illuminated that mind did it become truly profound. In the *Praise of Folly* Erasmus gave something that no one else could have given to the world.

The Modern Relevance of *The Praise of Folly*

by Robert P. Adams

Erasmus' *Praise of Folly*, famous throughout the Europe of its day, is still well enough known to need little introduction. Perhaps its gaiety and verve can be best enjoyed, however, when it is squarely set at the dawn of what the humanists in England hoped was to be a new Golden Age of peaceful social reconstruction. The whole tone of the piece is bracing, optimistic, and constructive. Like all first-rate satire, it seeks to expose and explode accumulations of human asininities; idiot structures must be blown down (preferably by laughter) to clear the ground—and the air—for new ones better suited to decent human aspiration. Satiric laughter of Erasmus' kind seeks also to clear out pockets of decay, to repair what is worth saving. "Folly," in Erasmus' sense, means, comprehensively, human fatuity—but fundamentally of the curable kinds. Such a satire is possible only at one of those historic moments when the writer, at least, really believes that, if reason is brought rightly to bear, the human animal can yet be brought to live wisely and well, in harmony with his kind and the world around him. Satire grows despairing and suicidal when—as with the older Swift— pessimism overwhelms perhaps writer and readers alike, when man's age-old fatuities have taken on the sinister aspect of massive insanities, and hope for achievement of a rational and humane social order flickers very low. T. S. Eliot's *The Waste Land*, Franz Kafka's *The Trial*, Aldous Huxley's *Brave New World*, Arthur Koestler's *Darkness at Noon*, George Orwell's *Animal Farm* and *1984* suggest this bleak and terrible temper for western Europe in the mid-twentieth century.

It is important to remember the obvious—that in 1509 the London Reformers did *not* know that, just over the horizon, were to come the Lutheran turmoils, the terrifyingly swift collapse of the old medieval order (or what remained of it), and the explosion of Europe into the wars of religion. In the bright England of 1509, almost any good thing seemed possible to achieve, given wit, hard work, and the requisite

"The Modern Relevance of The Praise of Folly*" (Editor's title). From* The Better Part of Valor: More, Erasmus, Colet and Vives on Humanism *by Robert P. Adams (Seattle: University of Washington Press, 1962), pp. 43–54. Copyright © 1962 by the University of Washington Press. Reprinted by permission of the publisher.*

royal leadership of a nobly Christian prince—Henry VIII. The *Praise of Folly* breathes an air of hope, of toleration, and of critical intelligence eager to be at work creating a peacefully reformed way of life. Whatever one may think of Erasmus as prophet in 1509, no one has ever been able to subject his satire to the fate of *Gulliver's Travels,* which has been turned into an innocently droll fairy tale for children. Like Swift and Thomas More—perhaps like all great humorists and ironists—Erasmus, beneath the mask of laughter, is quite serious.

For our story, the *Praise of Folly* is most fascinating for its trenchant and central satire on war and warmakers, past and present. Within the whole work this forms a structure of relentlessly ironic social criticism, both destructive and constructive. Erasmus was addressing himself to an audience which, if schooled in the quite usual medieval patterns of thought, customarily regarded war (like the plague) as caused by man's sin and God's answering justice, yet at the same time (since St. Augustine) as an action approvable as just and Christian. The accretions of chivalrous romance, moreover, had dressed war in a heroic glamour suitable for one of nobility's most glorious occupations. In startling contrast, Erasmus presented a Christian-humanist image of war and warmakers as beastly, hellish, corruptive of human society, unjust, and unchristian. War is not treated as an incurable form of human folly; it is not in the nature of things inevitable and necessary; it is corrupted men who make it so. The satire was designed progressively to amuse, surprise, shock, appall, and, finally, prompt pensive men to re-examine time-hallowed medieval values and authorities, then—as necessary—to modify and reform them through the right use of reason and the Scriptures.

Erasmus' general method used the personification of Folly as a mouthpiece through which to deliver a witty monologue and commentary upon a wide range of human affairs. Sustained ironic praise is skillfully applied to the manifold absurdities or traditionally established (but potentially alterable and curable) follies of human life. Common patterns of thought and feeling are amusedly held up for inspection in an uncommonly bright humorous light. The opening viewpoint is much like that echoed by Ben Jonson in the prologue to *Every Man in His Humour,* ninety years later. Presented are:

> . . . deeds . . ./ And persons, such as Comedy would choose,
> When she would shew an image of the times,
> And sport with human follies, not with crimes.
> Except we make them such, by loving still
> Our popular errors, when we know they're ill.
> I mean such errors as you'll all confess,
> By laughing at them, they deserve no less:
> Which when you heartily do, there's hope left then,
> You, that have so grac'd monsters, may like men.

The theme of war in the *Praise of Folly* is handled in three main divisions. First, mankind's martial and related proclivities (such as hunting) are ironically lauded as forming part of the general lunacy characteristic of civilization. Next—the attacks growing more specific and coming closer to home—the warmakings of popes and churchmen are treated. Finally, in the criticism of theologians who falsify Christ and the Scriptures to justify war, the whole movement rises to its climax, the grasp tightens, the mood becomes formidable, and that this Christian folly is, in Erasmus' view, "the most important thing he has to say, one cannot well doubt." [1]

To begin with, the satire against war is fairly general, as Folly laughs with amused sympathy at choice varieties of whimsical prejudice and national *amour-propre*. She represents herself to us as the greatest of all inventors, creator of "all noble acts and arts" which cultural historians praise. But of all these noble inventions the first, the greatest, the maddest, and the most profitless to man, was war: ". . . is not war the seed-plot and fountain of renowned actions? Yet what is more foolish than to enter upon a conflict for I know not what causes, wherein each side reaps more of loss than of gain?" How can the carcasses left on the battlefield receive any glory? "As for those who fall, as was said of the Megarians, 'no particulars.' " But is it not always said that wise men are essential for military planning? Call it what it is—"military, not philosophical, wisdom." Of little use would be true philosophy—i.e., concerned with knowing the truth, including how to live well. "Far otherwise: this famous game of war is played by parasites, panders, bandits, assassins, peasants, sots, bankrupts, and such other dregs of mankind." Having thus begun with the semi-paradox that wisdom is useless in war, Folly—with droll illustration—concludes that so-called wise men of peace are useless for all practical affairs (*EPF*, pp. 30–31).

From foolishness in general we move toward certain classes of folly large enough to take in the greater part of mankind—for instance, the custom of hunting, in which men everywhere find such joy. Erasmus' satire against hunting is an organic part of the mockery of war. In fact the theme of hunting is bound up with an apparently neo-Stoic theory devised to explain how primitive man may have fallen from the total peace which he enjoyed in the mythical golden age. As Folly sees such activities as hunting, their general characteristic

---

[1] H. H. Hudson in his edition of *The Praise of Folly* (Princeton, N. J., 1941), p. 130 (cited hereafter as *EPF*). As satirist of inventors, Folly of course seems to mock the Prometheus myth, in which invention is the key to "progress." Though more literally accurate, Hudson's translation lacks the vivid energy of the 1549 version by Sir Thomas Chaloner: *The Praise of Folly*, trans. Sir Thomas Chaloner, ed. J. Ashbee, London, 1921 (cited hereafter as *EPF-C*). See also *Encomium Moriae* (1515), facsimile edition by H. Schmid (Basel, 1931).

is that sheer custom has gradually so befuddled mankind that what is, to an objective observer (like Folly!), naturally hideous in itself has become transmuted into sheer joy. In their mutual delights, madmen laugh together. What droll fellows these hunters are! Happy in their delusions (like the ignorant cuckold who "flatters himself in the key of C-major"), as they hunt wild game, they:

> . . . feel an ineffable pleasure in their souls whenever they hear the raucous blast of the horns and the yelping of the hounds. Even the dung of the dogs, I am sure, smells like cinnamon to them. And what is so sweet as a beast being butchered? Cutting up bulls and oxen is properly given over to the humble plebeian, but it is a crime for game to be slaughtered except by a gentleman! There, with his head bared, on bended knees, with a knife designed just for this (for it is sacrilege to use any other), with certain ceremonial gestures he cuts just the proper members in the approved order. The company stands in silence, wondering as at some great novelty, although it has seen the same spectacle a thousand times. And if some bit of the animal is handed one of them to taste, he thinks he has gone up a step or so in the ranks of the nobility. And thus with their butchering and eating of beasts they accomplish nothing at all unless it be to degenerate into beasts themselves, though they think, all the while, they are living the life of a king [*EPF*, p. 53].

One wonders whether Erasmus had ever seen Henry VIII, for whom hunting was a passion, at his sport.

Already linked in Erasmus' thought on war are evidently at least three elements. One is that, earlier in history, man's inventive talents were misused by the invention of war itself—with its weapons, technologies, and ceremonies. Second, he observed the pleasure which contemporary men took in that miniature war, hunting. Third, he advanced the idea that, although the hunters are apparently happily unaware of it, what they have accomplished through habitual use of butchery is their own degeneration from the distinctively human toward the bestial. Evidently this reasoning process involves several simple presuppositions: that once upon a time man lived without war and without hunting; that in this earlier condition he lived in a fashion more admirably human, more perfect, than at present (when he unthinkingly enjoys butchery); that man is quite capable of so changing—from an earlier, uncorrupted state—until he is no longer consciously aware either that his tastes and habits are vile, or how vile they are ("the dung of the dogs smells like cinnamon to them"). What we have here seems to be a sketch toward a theory of history and of what might be termed progress. But Folly, through Erasmus' irony, attacks the entire process and holds it up to our view as one of degeneration. It was the ancient Prometheus myth which carried with it admiration for inventors; apparently Erasmus is not (here, at least) impressed unreservedly with the beauties of man's technological progress, including his invention

of the art of war. Erasmus will return to the entire theory of history
in his greatest piece of war criticism, the *Bellum Erasmi* (1515). Here
perhaps it is sufficient to mention only that his efforts, in the *Praise
of Folly*, to work out what I have termed a theory of history represent
a striking example of his humanism. For he not only absorbed favorite
classics (Lucretius, Ovid, Cicero, but above all Seneca and Plutarch),
but transmuted them so that they furnished power and light for the
English as well as European situation in 1509.[2]

The tone of the satire becomes grimmer when the attack centers
upon the warmaking of a degenerate papal hierarchy. The chief target
becomes easily recognizable when he devises "an undoubtedly serious
criticism of the Church as he had seen it in Italy under Julius II." [3]
As he warms to this theme, the irony becomes more brutal and the
tension so great that the work almost breaks into outright denuncia-
tion. The result suggests the intensity and hard realism which mark
the London Reformers' analysis of evil conditions whose reform
became daily more vital to Christendom. To the historical method
in criticism, Erasmus couples Lucianic irony and his own special form
of wit: the result is work distinctive of the Christian humanism then
emerging in England.

After a glancing cut at sycophantic courtiers and at kings who
ignored the duties of kinship, Folly's satirical eye rested on the great
princes of the Church. In general, contemporary cardinals compare
badly with the ancient apostles. Why cannot these cardinals muster up
enough purity and charity to work for the primitive Christian ends:
"teaching, exhorting, chastising, admonishing, ending wars, resisting
wicked princes, and freely spending blood—not money alone—for the
flock of Christ?" But what can one expect when, as of late, "popes,
cardinals, and bishops," after sedulous imitation, have almost beaten
the secular princes at their own games? Besides, if they were actually
to lead lives of Christian humility and poverty, think of the unem-
ployment that would result! What would become of "all those advocates, promoters, secretaries, muleteers, grooms, bankers, and pimps"
who now have steady employment (*EPF*, pp. 97–99)?

---

[2] See Lucretius *De rerum natura* v.988–1009; Ovid *Metamorphoses* i.76–215, and
Pythagoras' account, given by Ovid, *ibid.* xv.75–142; Seneca *Epistulae morales* 90.4–
16 etc.; Plutarch, "Of Eating Flesh (whether it be lawful or no)," *The Philosophie
. . . called, the Morals*, trans. P. Holland (London, 1603), pp. 572–74 *passim*. For
these texts and other classical parallels see LB, pp. 23–102, 263–79. In the essay cited,
Plutarch treats the beginning of bloodshed as dating from rupture of a presumed
primitive peace between men and beasts, after which men became progressively
brutalized, ending by enjoying what at first seemed cruel or "unnatural." Erasmus'
whole process of reasoning could easily be derived from Seneca: *Ep. mor.* 90.41,
108.17–20, 75.11–12; "A Treatise of Anger," *Workes*, trans. Lodge (London, 1614),
pp. 510–30 *passim; Ep. mor.* 94:61–66. Much similar reasoning appears in Seneca's
De beneficiis.

[3] W. E. Campbell, *Erasmus, Tyndale and More* (London, 1949), pp. 52–54.

The satire in the *Praise of Folly* grows still more intense and destructive when Folly considers the papacy. It would appear from her critique that it was no use looking now for St. Peter's apostolic virtues in the popes. Christian labor?—that "they hand over to Peter and Paul, who have leisure for it. But the splendor and the pleasure they take care of personally" (*EPF*, p. 99). They live in the grossest luxury and, worst of all, are devoted to the vice of war. Indeed their wars to gain and extend ill-gotten wealth have demoralized the Church, whose worst enemies such popes actually are. From them the name of Christ receives scant lip service, but the papal hand is always ready to whip out a sword and "stick it into the guts of his brother." The means which made the primitive Church grow strong—peace and self-sacrifice —are out of date. Nowadays the Pope's main business is to destroy anyone who (doubtless devilishly inspired) would reduce the "patrimony of Peter"—i.e., the vast wealth of the Church. And so they hurry to war: "On behalf of these things . . . they fight with fire and sword, not without shedding of Christian blood; and then they believe they have defended the bride of Christ in apostolic fashion." To war rush these "most holy fathers . . . and vicars of Christ"! No matter if war is more bestial than human, if it is hellish, if it blights morals like a plague, if it is unjust and the work of criminals, if it is truly unchristian:

> . . . nowadays they carry on Christ's cause by the sword. . . . And although war is so cruel a business that it befits beasts and not men, so frantic [*insana*] that poets feign it is sent with evil purpose by the Furies, so pestilential that it brings with it a general blight upon morals, so iniquitous that it is usually conducted by the worst bandits [*pessimis latronibus*], so impious that it has no accord with Christ, yet our popes, neglecting all their other concerns, make it their only task.

Of course the "mob of priests, forsooth, consider it a sacrilege to fall short of their prelates in holiness. O brave! They war on behalf of their right to tithe in the best military manner, with swords, darts, stones and forces of arms" (*EPF*, pp. 100–1).

No contemporary of Erasmus' was likely to mistake the chief target of this attack for any but Julius II:

> Here [on the war scene] you will see feeble old men [Chaloner expanded this: "so old and wasted, that their bones rattle in their skins"] assuming the strength of youth, not shocked by the expense or tired out by the labor, not at all discouraged, if only they may upset laws, religion, peace, and all humane usages, and turn them heels over head.

Nor will the pope lack "learned sycophants" who will sanction such vile wars with pious texts:

> Who will give to this manifest madness [*manifestariam insaniam*] the names of zeal, piety, and fortitude, devising a way whereby it is possible for a man to whip out his sword, stick it into the guts of his brother, and

nonetheless dwell in that supreme charity which, according to Christ's precept, a Christian owes to his neighbor [*EPF,* p. 101].

Thus did Erasmus' *Praise of Folly* represent the old Pope Julius who, in Ranke's words, "from the tumults of a general war . . . hoped to extract the fulfillment of his purposes . . . to be the lord and master of the game of the world." [4] Winding up this savage indictment, Erasmus has Folly at once ironically disclaim the slightest intention to "rattle up the vices" of any living Churchman. And of course Folly only praises bad men, whom she likes to eulogize, but she had better say so lest someone think the *Praise of Folly* to be satiric (*EPF,* p. 103; *EPF-C,* p. 69)!

The last target of the satire that matters here is Erasmus' treatment of the traditional scholastic interpretation of Scripture by which, since St. Augustine's day, war had been justified. Unmistakably in this work he carried on what Colet had begun in his 1496 lectures on St. Paul at Oxford, using the same historical method in criticism but using it with superior flexibility, insight, and wit. This was deeply serious to Erasmus, and while the irony deepens toward the tragic, the passage tends to abandon the light and jocund tone with which he initiated his high-spirited, humorous mock eulogy of human fatuity.

The literary climax of Erasmus' lifework was to be his edition of the New Testament—the *Novum instrumentum* of 1516—work largely done in England and doubtless in his plans when in 1509 he came to England to live, with every apparent intention of making it his permanent home. In 1496 Colet had searched for the original, primitive meaning of the Scriptures, largely bypassing the scholastic commentators. This whole vital question of biblical interpretation could not very long be separated from the question of a text whose editing would include the latest advances in scholarship.

When in the *Praise of Folly,* therefore, Folly began to cite Scripture to bolster her authority in the world of deluded men, the satire rapidly came to a focus sharply on the question of the biblical authority for terming war to be just. Potentially there were few more explosive subjects for critical investigation; for when this is followed far enough, inevitably one is led to re-examine the basis and justice of power, monarchic or ecclesiastic.

At first Folly seems very pleased; ironically she affects to feel quite at home with these subtle scholastics, so clever and ingenious in reading meaning into the Scriptures. It's no less than "magistral"! Why, these days the "sons of theologues" can prove anything to their own purpose. The secret of their method, it seems, is to pluck out four or five little words "from here and there, even depraving the sense of

[4] L. von Ranke, *The History of the Popes,* trans. E. Foster (London, 1889), I, 40–41.

them, if need be; although the words which precede and follow these are nothing at all to the point or even go against it." In short, by these critical devices (Folly applauds), scriptural precepts are mutilated and abridged, wrenched from their context, and so in the end readily found to mean something quite contrary to the example of Christ's own life. By such methods, indeed, "I pray you . . . tell me, what thing may be too hard for these doctors to bring about?" (*EPF*, p. 33).

For her part, Folly, using the example of Christ's conduct shortly before his death, admits to such stupidity that, to her, it seems Christ meant Christians to shun weapons and violence. Knowing the end to be near, Christ told his apostles to provide themselves with swords as needed in their mission of spreading the gospel. What did this counsel mean? To Folly (who resorts to historical criticism of a simple kind) the meaning is clear enough, in the context of Christ's whole life and teaching. The apostles were to secure and employ "not the sword with which bandits and murderers attack, but the sword of the spirit. . . ." Ah! but not so, says the scholastic expositor. To him (says Folly with some of Erasmus' bitterest irony) it is all quite different. It seems that Christ's injunctions of nonviolence really mean that his apostles should be armed to the teeth with all the latest military weapons. (Updating, Erasmus supplies "muskets.") Similarly the small knapsack of supplies that Christ had in mind is metamorphosed into a whole baggage train of fine food. Nor is such a critic at all disturbed "that He who thus earnestly bade that a sword be purchased, soon after with a rebuke ordered the same weapon to be sheathed; or that no one has ever heard it told that the apostles used swords or shield against the violence of the heathen . . ." though presumably they would have done so had Christ so intended.[5]

The satire ends on a note of serious humor. Is it possible that Christianity itself has some deep "kinship with some sort of folly"? Just ponder the huge discrepancy between Christ's life and those lived by many of his professed modern followers! Many? A majority! And naturally, by majority vote, the minority (who seek to use Christ's whole life as their guide) can easily be declared quite mad. As for Folly, she always agrees with the majority. Why not? They are her faithful devotees. Encouraging readers to "applaud . . . live . . . drink," Erasmus' figure of Folly bids a fond farewell to a world crammed with fascinating lunacies (*EPF*, pp. 118–25).

The *Praise of Folly* (like More's *Utopia*) has often been termed a *jeu d'esprit*, and so it is. But it is much more than that, for it marks a tremendous forward step in social criticism. This is no shaft politely released from some Renaissance ivory tower. It belongs to world literature, true, but the satire's roots run deep into its own time. As critic Erasmus now permanently took his place as a man committed to aiding

[5] *EPF*, pp. 111–13 *passim;* Matthew 26:52, Mark 14:47, Luke 22:50.

humanist reforms, not as one outside, a genial spectator, but as a fighter in the midst of a fateful struggle for a better social order, and as one passionately engaged in the great movement of the age.

As criticism, moreover, the work marks an immense growth in the structure of ideas. Summing up, Erasmus put forward five major points about war, points which link his attack to the search for vital reforms of Christendom. First, he argues that war is beastly, that is, more befitting the true, uncorrupted nature of beasts than of men. Here he revives and gives new impetus to the classical beast-man comparisons and analyses. But he is not content merely to echo certain classics, giving the satire a neo-Stoic cast. What he opens out, tentatively, is a critical inquiry into what may be a tragic dichotomy in human nature. Why is man, a creature of such wondrous natural and divine endowments, potentially "a little lower than the angels," seemingly (at least) capable of life ruled by reason and love, prone (as in war) to actions so vile? Why is this creature at times worse than any animal? "A beast without reason," Hamlet will mourn (confronted with another fall from ideal humanity) "would have mourned longer." The whole idea is central in English Renaissance tragedy. But, in the *Praise of Folly*, Erasmus is not content to offer the standard medieval answer, that the cause of this tragic fall is man's sin. Rather, as humanist, he examines intensely man's capacities for irrational and antihuman behavior. Clearly all this involves an implicit theory of what man's capacities for a good life actually are, as well as of means for its realization. This whole complex of thought will be more fully explored in the London Reformers' later social criticism, most fully by More and Vives.

The idea that war is bestial, however, may be a libel on the beasts. Secondly, Erasmus raises the view that war is hellish—"so frantic [*insana*] that poets feign it is sent with evil purpose by the Furies." This carries us toward a tragic perspective exceeding the first. Erasmus, nevertheless, again puts the idea in a humanistic and poetic rather than simply some traditional theological frame. The "devil theory" of historical causation has, to be sure, long had its advocates.[6] Erasmus' way of raising the question invites deep reflection upon the interaction of reason and unreason (or sheer passion and overwhelming compulsions able to topple reason, as when men go berserk with mass-murderous fury) within the nature of man. Shakespeare's plebeians, listening with respect to Brutus' explanation of why he slew Caesar for the good of Rome, seem to be reasonable men. Mark Antony knows the potential vileness of human nature better than the too uncritically stoical Brutus, knows what these same Romans will do in frenzy when he has worked upon them, what unspeakable horrors will be commonplace when this hellish element is released (as perhaps periodically—we might say subconsciously—many men hope it may sometime be) when

---

[6] See C. A. Beard, *The Devil Theory of War* (New York, 1936).

"Caesar's spirit, ranging for revenge, / With Ate by his side, come hot from hell," is given free play at the most fearful of all Renaissance military commands: "Havoc!" In the *Praise of Folly* Erasmus marks the line of insight which points toward Shakespeare's *Julius Caesar*.

Third, Erasmus advances the idea that war is "so pestilential that it brings with it a general blight upon morals." Thus he suggests the analogy of war and disease. The analogy invites the critical mind to search for causes, prompts again a search into the "nature" of man and the forces at work in his natural environment, an inquiry most imaginatively to be carried out by More in his *Utopia* and by Vives in his latest works.

The fourth and fifth points are closely related in the *Praise of Folly* —that war is unjust and unchristian. Pursuit of both these themes leads toward sharp re-examination, not only of orthodox medieval doctrines of the Church, but of the uses (and abuses) of monarchic and papal powers. Every one of these ideas was potentially dynamite.

To be sure, in the *Praise of Folly*, while these five ideas are all present, some remain in a germinal state. Very probably, at this stage, Erasmus himself had not fully worked out his thought on war and social reform. Nevertheless, as humanist criticism of life, the *Praise of Folly* marks a substantial advance. Barely twenty-five years earlier, in Caxton's work, we moved in a medieval landscape; but now in Erasmus the scene, the very air—the ideas and their attached emotions—all are predominantly distinguished by a changed and Renaissance outlook. The *Praise of Folly*, moreover, appeals for both reflection and action. During the decade to follow, More, Erasmus, Colet, and their friends will (as voyagers of the mind) on the one hand follow out these five ideas and others, discovering many curious ramifications. On the other, being humanists concerned with the search for a good life in both practice and theory, they will be found busy in practical efforts to help design and construct a new social order in England.

In this total humanist effort, every literary and practical talent the London Reformers possessed will be stretched to the utmost. One of the most potent instruments for appealing to men of reason is irony. It has been already suggested that, in their 1505–6 translations from Lucian, More and Erasmus began to bring irony into modern literature. Until now I have used the term "Lucianic irony" to denote this trait, but it becomes inadequate. For, in the *Praise of Folly*, Erasmus demonstrates command of a form of irony distinctive of himself and his friend More, an irony dramatically far advanced over Lucian's.[7] "Erasmian irony" is perhaps the best term available. This irony and its frequent companion, humor, mark much of these humanists' best work in the decade of optimism, after 1509, when a golden age of peaceful reform seemed achievable in England.

[7] See Leonard Dean in his translation of *The Praise of Folly* (Chicago, 1946), pp. 16–30.

The Ironic Mock Encomium

by Walter Kaiser

The rubric, *Stultitia loquitur,* that stands at the head of the *Moriae encomium* announces what is the most important single fact about Erasmus' book. It ought to come as something of a surprise, and surely it did to its first readers; for nothing in the title or the epistle dedicatory prepares us for the fact that this encomium of folly is to be delivered by Folly herself. There is, indeed, no precedent for it in the literary tradition. The title of the book, though intentionally somewhat oxymoronic, cannot have come as any great surprise to the intelligent, well-read reader of 1511. There would doubtless have been a certain amusement in finding that Brandt's ship, launched less than two decades before, had been sailed so triumphantly into port, but the mock-encomiastic genre was not unfamiliar, and the reader would probably have recalled at once that long tradition of works which praised "Busireses, Phalarises, quartan fevers, flies, baldness, and plagues of that sort." To have found that it is Folly herself who speaks may have occasioned some greater surprise, especially since in Brandt's book it was Wisdom who occupied the pulpit and preached admonishingly to the fools sitting beneath her. Moreover, as some readers may have remembered, the one time that one of Brandt's fools did mount to the pulpit, he was struck dumb.[1] Yet actually, for the ridiculous to speak was no less traditional than for the ridiculous to be praised: like the vicious and the bestial, the ridiculous and foolish had early won the right of speech in literature.

What would have been astonishing to the reader of 1511, however, is the fact that here the ridiculous is praising itself. Fools had spoken before this and foolishness had been praised; but never before had a fool praised foolishness. Erasmus' great originality, then, was to make Stultitia both the author and the subject of her encomium, to con-

---

"The Ironic Mock Encomium." From Praisers of Folly: Erasmus, Rabelais, Shakespeare *by Walter Kaiser (Cambridge, Mass.: Harvard University Press, 1963), pp. 35–50. Copyright, 1963, by the President and Fellows of Harvard College. Reprinted by permission of the publisher.*

[1] Sebastian Brandt, *The Ship of Fools,* tr. Alexander Barclay, ed. T. H. Jamieson (Edinburgh and London, 1874; 2 vols.), I, 119; II, 273, 231.

ceive of "Moriae" as being simultaneously both objective and subjective genitive. Thus, "The Praise of Folly" only translates half of the title: it might more accurately be rendered as "Folly's Praise of Folly."

As Erasmus' title thus doubles back on itself, it tends to cancel itself out in the fashion of a double negative. At least one is already tantalized by the doubt that it may cancel itself out. Or is it perhaps actually a triple negative? Does doubt cancel out doubt? To begin to examine the problem is to condemn oneself to a vertiginous semantic labyrinth. For the praise of folly, being a *mock* praise, is in fact the censure of folly; but if Folly is thus censuring folly, Wisdom would presumably praise folly. Or, to look at it from another angle, if the praise of folly is, by its mock-encomiastic nature, actually the praise of wisdom, Folly must be praising wisdom. But if Folly praises wisdom, then Wisdom would presumably censure wisdom. One is obliged to surrender to the manner of Gertrude Stein and say: to praise folly is fooling, but if Folly is foolish and Folly is praising folly, then the foolish is fooling— that is, wisdom is being praised. Yet, if the unwise is praising wisdom, it is folly to do so, and wisdom to praise folly. If the reader is by now thoroughly lost, I am not surprised. Nor, for that matter, would Erasmus be; for it is in just this way that he intended to confuse his reader. The simplest statement of his strategy—that Folly praises folly—propounds an insoluble dilemma of permanent uncertainty similar to the famous statement of St. Paul that Epimenides the Cretan said Cretans always lie.[2]

Erasmus' book is a mock encomium—but at the same time the mocking is mocked. I know of no other mock encomium before the *Moriae encomium* that employs this subtle device,[3] and after Erasmus only Swift successfully approximates it. Certain modern authors have at times done something analogous, and there are common dramatic devices that are often very similar, but, with the exception of Swift, no one has employed this particular strategy in quite the way Erasmus does. It would therefore seem likely that Erasmus did more than rein-

---

[2] The complex structure and effect of such ironic ambiguities have interesting and illuminating analogues in the visual arts; and insofar as the ironic mode dictates and is dependent upon a certain perspective or "point of view," it is perhaps not without significance that Erasmus develops this new type of irony at precisely the same time that Dürer and others are experimenting with the science of visual perspective. The work done by Panofsky and other art historians is indispensable for any examination of this relationship, and I should also like to refer the interested reader to the brilliant book by E. H. Gombrich, *Art and Illusion. A Study in the Psychology of Pictorial Representation* (New York, 1960). Gombrich's third section, "The Beholder's Share" (pp. 181–287), offers particularly suggestive analogies to Erasmus' irony.

[3] For an ample collection of these, see Caspar Dornavius, ed., *Amphitheatrum Sapientiae Socraticae Joco-seriae, hoc est, Encomia et Commentaria Autorum, qua veterum, qua recentiorum prope omnium: quibus Res, aut pro vilibus vulgo aut damnosis habitae, Styli Patrocinio vindicantur, exornantur* . . . (Hanover, 1619).

troduce sustained irony into European literature. He appears, in fact,
to have invented a new kind of irony.

When this has been said, however, it must still be admitted that
there is one particular probable inspiration, if not direct source, for
the kind of irony Erasmus has created. Though we find nothing like it
in other mock encomia, we do find something very similar in the
thought of the most prominent pagan in Erasmus' hagiarchy, Socrates.
There is a passage in the *Apology*, which will be examined in greater
detail when we consider Rabelais, that comes astonishingly close to
the technique of the *Encomium*: this is the passage about the oracle at
Delphi, where Socrates claims he is the wisest of men because he knows
that he is ignorant. It is not surprising that Stultitia herself gives evidence of having read this Platonic work and recalls this specific passage.[4] At one point in her eulogy, Stultitia observes that what she is
saying may at first sight seem foolish or absurd, and yet it is really
profoundly true.[5] Few single sentences in the *Encomium* demonstrate
more clearly the puzzle of Chinese boxes that Erasmian irony contains.
Stultitia says that what seem to be her absurdities are actually truths.
Yet, because Stultitia says it, it may not be so, since the truth of Stultitia may be foolishness. But in that case, the foolishness of Stultitia
ought to be truth; and perhaps what Erasmus is saying is: "What at
first sight may seem true is really absurd." How can we tell which
he means? The answer is that he means neither one nor the other, but
both, and more than both. One cannot reduce Erasmian irony, any
more than one can Socratic irony, to a simple formula; even the complex statement of the mechanics of this irony two paragraphs above is a
dangerous oversimplification. Folly is foolish and Folly is wise, but
the head of Janus is greater than both of his faces. One might, indeed,
propound as a general theory the fact that the highest tropes operate
on a formula of one plus one equals three. Empson has demonstrated
this to be true of ambiguity, and students of the drama know that the
meaning of a play is greater than the sum of the "meanings" of the
characters. So, in the same way, the greatest works of art (as Socrates
seems to suggest at the end of the *Symposium*) incorporate both the
comic and the tragic visions but inhabit a higher sphere than either.
If Dorp, Erasmus' first critic, misread the *Encomium* by taking every
statement literally, later critics have often misread it as badly by
taking every statement for its opposite. Either position tends to miss
the point; and we cannot really understand the *Encomium* until we
see the truth and realize the implications of a recent critic's observation
that in the *Praise of Folly*, irony "does more than affect the meaning.
There theme and tone blend: the irony *becomes* the meaning." [6]

    [4] Plato, *Apologia Socratis*, 21A–22E. Cf. ME 38.
    [5] ME 64: "Rem dicam prima fronte stultam fortassis atque absurdam, sed tamen
unam multo verissimam."
      [6] C. R. Thompson, tr., *Ten Colloquies of Erasmus* (New York, 1957), p. xxii.

That Erasmus should have written his most famous book in this manner should not be surprising. The man who attacked both the Church and the Church's attacker at the same time, who urged that Luther be protected by the princes but refused to side with Luther, who placed Socrates in the same order of the blessed with St. Paul, obviously conceived that truth was rarely simple. His biographer Huizinga has emphasized:

> If Erasmus so often hovers over the borderline between earnestness and mockery, if he hardly ever gives an incisive conclusion, it is not only due to cautiousness, and fear to commit himself. Everywhere he sees the shadings, the blending of the meaning of words. The terms of things are no longer to him, as to the man of the Middle Ages, as crystals mounted in gold, or as stars in the firmament. "I like assertions so little that I would easily take sides with the sceptics wherever it is allowed by the inviolable authority of Holy Scripture and the decrees of the Church." "What is exempt from error?" [7]

Georges Duhamel signalizes this same quality in Erasmus when he writes, "I would readily call him 'the king of *but*.'" [8] Surely such apparent vacillation is rather a quality of the maturest minds: the ability to see both sides of a question implies a particularly high order of wisdom.[9] Yet the tragedy of Erasmus' life lay exactly here, in this quality of mind that was incomprehensible to his contemporaries. One would not, of course, have expected comprehension, much less toleration, of Erasmus' position from either Luther at one extreme or the monks of Spain at the other; but even his friend Dürer one day entered in his journal the poignant cry, "O Erasmus roterodamus, wo willst du bleiben?" [10] The Luthers could assert, "Hier stehe ich!" but Erasmus, had he heard Dürer's question, could only have answered, "Here *I* stand—but also here, and here, and here." So, too, his mouthpiece Stultitia is ambiguously vacillatory, unsure even of what is folly and what is wisdom: "I wyst there was none of you all so wyse, or rather so foolysshe, naie wyse sooner, as wolde be of any other opinion." [11] The concepts are confused and blurred, until we cannot tell

[7] J. Huizinga, *Erasmus of Rotterdam*, tr. F. Hopman (London, 1952), p. 116.

[8] Georges Duhamel, *Deux Patrons* (Paris, 1937), p. 33. H. R. Trevor-Roper has more recently given a sensitive appreciation of just this quality of equipollence in Erasmus' mind, in *Historical Essays* (London, 1957), pp. 35–60.

[9] Cf. Whitehead's interesting remark: "Now what, *exactly*, did Plato mean? He was at pains *never* to mean anything exactly. He gave every side of a question its due. I have often done the same, advancing some aspect which I thought deserved attention, and then in some later work, presenting its opposite. In consequence I am accused of inconsistency and self-contradiction." *Dialogues of Alfred North Whitehead as Recorded by Lucien Price* (New York, Mentor Books, 1956), p. 247.

[10] *Dürers Schriftlicher Nachlass auf Grund der Originalhandschriften und Theilweise neu entdeckter alter Abschriften*, ed. K. Lange and F. Fuhse (Halle am Salle, 1893), p. 164.

[11] ME 16: "Equidem sciebam, neminem vestrum ita sapere, vel desipere magis, imo sapere potius, ut in hac esset sententia."

them apart. Even Listrius loses his customary confidence in interpreting this particular sentence.[12] Yet whatever conclusion we come to, the sentence still seems to say that to make a mistake is to be wise. But then, of course, this is said by Stultitia, a fool. And so we find ourselves once again lost in the labyrinth.

The substitution by the Renaissance humanists of rhetorical for syllogistic argumentation is a phenomenon which has often been attested to. It is enough merely to observe here that Stultitia's role as orator and her claim that oratory is the least mendacious mirror of the mind are indicative of her Erasmianism; indeed, her very phrase (*oratio, minime mendax animi speculum*) is stolen from Erasmus' *Apophthegmata*, where he derives the idea from Socrates via Xenophon.[13] Accordingly, when she steps up to the pulpit, Stultitia launches into an oration which is classical in form, and no point is more labored by her at the beginning of her speech than that she is *not* going to give a scholastic dissertation. Hoyt Hudson demonstrated that the form of her speech adheres closely to the paradigm of oratorical structure expounded by Quintilian,[14] although, as we shall see, it is even closer to Greek models for encomia than to Roman models for public addresses. Accepting for the moment, however, the Quintilian paradigm, we can observe how Stultitia's speech begins with an exordium, moves through a narration and partition to the confirmation (which comprises the main body of the speech), and ends with the traditional peroration. In a typical gesture, Stultitia herself mocks the same form later in her speech when she attacks the sermons of the monks. Equally typical of her point of view are her substitution of an anti-partition for the partition and her sarcastic attacks on those who sprinkle such orations with Greek tags, a device which she herself will employ throughout her encomium, even the Greek title of which is also exposed to her ridicule.[15]

Discounting the partition, which is devoted to her refusal to give a partition, the exordium and narration comprise an introduction. In it she introduces the main themes that will inform the rest of the work.

[12] LB IV.412F: "Quanto cum decoro personae, variat correctionem? Porro quod aliis est desipere, id est Stultitiae, sapere."

[13] ME 6; cf. LB IV.162D (*Apophthegmata*). This idea will in turn be borrowed by two later Erasmians, Juan Luis Vives, who expanded it in his *De Ratione Dicendi* (*Opera* [Basle, 1555], pp. 103–5), and Ben Jonson, who Englished it out of Vives to supply his *Timber* with the celebrated passage beginning "*Language* most shewes a man: speake that I may see thee. It springs out of the most retired, and inmost parts of us, and is the Image of the Parent of it, the mind. No glasse renders a mans forme, or likenesse, so true as his speech" (Jonson, *Works*, VIII, 625).

[14] H. H. Hudson, tr., *The Praise of Folly by Desiderius Erasmus* (Princeton, 1941), pp. 129–42.

[15] ME 108: "cum in omnium paginarum frontibus leguntur tria nomina, praesertim peregrina . . ."

She begins by describing herself, and it is doubtless significant that the first thing she says—characteristically worded as a double negative—is that she is not ignorant: *neque enim sum nescia.* The opening sentence, in its Ciceronian length and elegance, introduces so many of the book's devices and techniques that it is worth considering in some detail.[16]

> Howe so ever men commonly talke of me (as pardie I am not ignoraunt what lewde reportes go on FOLIE, yea even amonges those that are veriest fooles of all) yet that I am she, l onely (I saie) who through myne influence do gladde both the Goddes and men, by this it maie appeare sufficiently: that as soone as I came forth to saie my mynd afore this your so notable assemblie, by and by all your lokes began to clere up: unbendyng the frounyng of your browes, & laughyng upon me with so merie a countinaunce, as by my trouth me semeth evin, that all ye (whom I see here present) doe fare as if ye were well whitled, and thoroughly moysted with the *Nectar* wine of the Homericall Goddes, not without a porcion of the juyce of that mervaillous herbe *Nepenthes,* whiche hath force to put sadnesse and melancholie from the herte: Where as before ye satte all heavie, and glommyng, as if ye had come lately from Trophonius cave . . .

It is appropriate that this speech, which is to destroy so many illusions, should thus begin with an *utcunque loquuntur* clause which places Folly in direct opposition to commonly accepted opinions, implies that those opinions are foolish (*stultissimos*), and insists upon the intelligence (*neque enim sum nescia*), uniqueness (*hanc inquam esse unam*), popularity (*hunc coetum frequentissimum*), and superiority (*meo numine deos atque homines exhilaro*) of Stultitia herself. It is characteristic that she proves her argument with a dubious proof which, upon further consideration, seems to have some validity after all—as John Donne, who recalled it, also insisted;[17] for while we may

---

[16] [In all cases where a passage is quoted in English and the original text is given in the note, the footnote numbers for such texts are given just before the English quotation so that the original text will begin at the bottom of the same page.] ME 1–2: "Utcunque de me vulgo mortales loquuntur, neque enim sum nescia, quam male audiat stultitia etiam apud stultissimos, tamen hanc esse, hanc inquam esse unam, quae meo numine deos atque homines exhilaro, vel illud abunde magnum est argumentum, quod simulatque in hunc coetum frequentissimum dictura prodii, sic repente omnium vultus nova quadam atque insolita hilaritate enituerunt, sic subito frontem exporrexistis, sic laeto quodam et amabili applausistis risu, ut mihi profecto quotquot undique praesentes intueor, pariter deorum Homericorum nectare, non sine nepenthe temulenti esse videamini, cum antehac tristes ac solliciti sederitis, perinde quasi nuper e Trophonii specu reversi."

[17] John Donne, *Paradox X:* "I always did, and shall understand that *Adage;*

per risum multum possis cognoscere stultum,

That by much *laughing* thou maist know there is a *fool,* not that the *laughers* are *fools,* but that among them there is some *fool,* at whom *wise men* laugh: which moved *Erasmus* to put this as his first *Argument* in the mouth of his *Folly,* that

question *amabili* (they are, obviously, laughing at her, not with her),
we cannot question *risu* (they *are* laughing). It is typical that in one
sentence she should employ a quotation from a Latin playwright
(Terence), a Greek poet (Homer), and even one from Erasmus' own
Adagia.[18] It is, finally, indicative of the message she is to propound
that she should, at the very outset of her speech, take it for granted
that gaiety and drunkenness are to be extolled and that sadness and
the melancholy effects of religion (the Delphic oracle of Zeus Tropho-
nius) should be deplored.

With the quasi-Lucretian description of spring in the next sentence,
Stultitia introduces the images of sunshine, vernality, and pleasure
with which she is repeatedly to characterize herself in her encomium.
She then proceeds to announce that it is her pleasure to play the
sophist for a while—not, she insists, the pedantic kind of sophist who
is nowadays the bane of schoolboys, but that ancient kind who took
the name Sophist to avoid the infamous name Wise.[19] Though Listrius
gives his customary explanation of this remark by ascribing it to the
decorum personae, we recognize the usual method in Stultitia's madness. Similarly when, several sentences later, she calls herself the true
bestower of all good things, we may recall that in the *Enchiridion*
Erasmus had applied an almost identical epithet, from the apochryphal
Wisdom of Solomon, to "the wisdom of Christ which the world thinks
folly." [20] Stultitia then explains that she is to praise herself in the
speech she will make, and she takes a swipe at those wise ones
(*sapientes istos*) who claim it is foolish for a person to praise himself.
Even if it is, she asks wittily, what could be more in character (*modo
decorum*)?

Following the traditional Quintilian order, Stultitia then proceeds
to the partition. In the land of medieval oratory, this particular plot
of ground was reserved especially for the encampment of the Schoolmen; the *genius loci* was Petrus Hispanus, the tourneys held there were
combats by choplogic. All that the humanist spirit hated most seemed
to be centered here in *divisiones* and *definitiones*, and it was the partition that was most commonly attacked or avoided in humanist ora-

---

she made Beholders laugh; for *fools* are the most laughed at, and laugh the least
themselves of any." *The Complete Poetry and Selected Prose of John Donne,* ed.
Charles M. Coffin (New York, Modern Library, 1952), pp. 286–7.

[18] See LB II.316E; Homer, *Odyssey,* IV.220–1; and LB II.292F–294B.

[19] ME 3: "Lubitum est enim paulisper apud vos Sophistam agere non quidem
hujus generis, quod hodie nugas quasdam anxias inculcat pueris, ac plusquam
muliebrem rixandi pertinaciam tradit, sed veteres illos imitabor, qui, quo infamem
Sophorum appellationem vitarent, *Sophistae* vocari maluerunt."

[20] E 40: "De Christi vero sapientia, quam mundus stultitiam putat, ita legis: *Vene-
runt autem mihi pariter omnia bona cum illa et innumerabilis honestas per manus
illius*" [*Sap.* 7.11].

tory.[21] Stultitia's scornful passing nod at the partition may be quoted in full.[22]

> But at my hand, ye shall heare an unadvised, and sodeine tale tolde, thoughe so muche perhaps the truer, Whiche I woulde not ye shoulde thynke were saied of me for a colour, to advaunce therby the rypenesse of my witte, as commonly these learned men do. Who puttyng foorthe (as ye knowe) some boke more than whole .xxx. wynters had in cullyng, ye and that sometymes none of their owne doyng, will sweare yet, that they made it but for a recreacion of theyr graver studies, or rather as fast as penne coulde renne. For truly it hath ever best lyked me to speake streight what so ever laie on my tongues ende. But this, to the ende ye loke not for it, I doe warne ye of afore hande, that I in no wyse will, accordyng to these common Sophisters and Rhetoriciens maner, go about to shew by deffinicion what I am, and muche lesse use any division: In as muche as I holde bothe the one, and the other for unluckie tokens, either to comprehende hir under a certaine ende, or limite, whose influence stretcheth so universally, orels to divide hir, in whose observaunce all men dooe so wholly consent. And yet I can not tell to what purpose it shoulde serve, to represent a certaine shadow, or image of my selfe, where as presently ye maie discerne me with your eies. For I am here (as ye see) the distributrix and dealer of all felicitee, named Μωρία in Greeke, in Latine *Stultitia,* in Englishe Folie.

Stultitia here insists upon the spontaneous and unlabored quality of her oration, much as Erasmus had insisted upon those same qualities in his book. Indeed, she pokes fun at the very excuses Erasmus had used in the epistle dedicatory to More and was to use again in the letter to Dorp: "tamen triduo sibi quasi per lusum scriptam." What was an excuse from Erasmus, however, becomes a militant defense from Stultitia. At pains throughout this brief partition to insist that spontaneity is truth, she utters whatever enters her head and draws attention to what she had earlier called "the mere sight of me" (*solo*

---

[21] For all of this, one may now consult Father Ong's monumental treatise on Ramus; for the humanist attack on Peter of Spain, see esp. ch. 4. Walter J. Ong, *Ramus, Method and the Decay of Dialogue* (Cambridge, Mass., 1958).

[22] ME 5–6: "A me extemporariam quidem illam et illaboratam, sed tanto veriorem audietis orationem. Id quod nolim existimetis ad ingenii ostentationem esse confictum, quemadmodum vulgus Oratorum facit. Nam ii, sicuti nostis, cum orationem totis triginta annis elaboratam, nonnunquam et alienam proferunt, tamen triduo sibi quasi per lusum scriptam, aut etiam dictatam esse dejerant. Mihi porro semper gratissimum fuit, ὅττι κεν ἐπὶ γλῶτταν ἔλθοι, dicere. At ne quis jam a nobis exspectet, ut juxta vulgarium istorum Rhetorum consuetudinem me ipsam finitione explicem; porro ut dividam, multo minus. Nam utrumque ominis est inauspicati, vel fine circumscribere eam, cuius numen tam late pateat, vel secare, in cuius cultum omne rerum genus ita consentiat. Tametsi quorsum tandem attinet mei velut umbram atque imaginem finitione repraesentare, cum ipsam me coram praesentes praesentem oculis intueamini? Sum etenim uti videtis, vera illa largitrix ἐάων quam Latini STULTITIAM, Graeci ΜΩΡ'ΙΑΝ appellant."

statim aspectu) rather than to any representation of herself. The function of this argument is the same as that of the epistle dedicatory: it obviates a riposte from the Schoolmen by refusing to compete on their grounds. It is all a game, and one can hardly deem the work serious enough to call for an answer. At the same time, there is a more positive aspect to this argument, for Stultitia is also claiming a certain value in naturalness, a certain truth in spontaneity.

Her next argument is akin to this. What is the point, she asks, of my even speaking, when you can see me for yourselves and my appearance is so unmistakable? "As if some one contendyng that I were Minerva, or Sophia, myght not straight with my onely loke be confuted . . . For in me (ye must thynke) is no place for settyng of colours [cosmetics], as I can not saie one thyng, and thynke an other." [23] Cosmetics (*fuci*) are as offensive to her as they are to Hamlet or Dean Swift or almost any of the great satirists. What is more, she pointedly implies that they are the property of Wisdom, as this world knows it. The suppositions, ampliations, restrictions, and appellations that we normally find in the partition are the cosmetics of the Schoolmen, and they are, as More wrote to Martin Dorp, not only inept but false.[24] The scholars, the Schoolmen, are said to be wise, but they are really hypocrites and *môrotatoi*, most foolish. May we not indeed, Stultitia asks, call them *môrosophoi?*—a word that Chaloner was to render for all time as "foolelosophers." Thus Stultitia uses a partition to refuse to deliver a partition, and more telling than her revelation of the hypocrisy of the Schoolmen is her demonstration of their futility. How, she asks, can you force into the bounds of a definition what is universal? How can you divide what is integral? She is speaking, of course, of the cult of folly. But—and the implication is unmistakable—she might just as well be speaking of the *cultus Christi*. It is the more devastating that she should attack the Schoolmen with their own favorite weapon, the partition, since by rejecting that particular oratorical device she has rejected the very basis of all their endeavors.

It is not only the Schoolmen who find themselves under her attack, however. She makes equal fun of the "nostri temporis rhetores," the humanist scholars. In doing so, she ridicules by implication Erasmus himself. "I have thought good to borowe," she says of her coinage *môrosophoi*, "a littell of the Rhetoriciens of these daies, who plainely thynke theim selves demygodes, if . . . thei can shew two tongues."

[23] ME 6: "aut quasi si quis me Minervam aut Sophiam esse contendat, non statim solo possit obtutu coargui, etiam si nulla accedat oratio, minime mendax animi speculum. Nullus apud me fucis locus, nec aliud fronte simulo, aliud in pectore premo."

[24] *The Correspondence of Sir Thomas More*, ed. E. F. Rogers (Princeton, 1947), p. 38: "in suppositionibus quas vocant in ampliationibus, restrictionibus, appellationibus, et vbi non quam ineptas, quam etiam falsas praeceptiunculas habet . . ." Cited in translation in Ong, *Ramus*, pp. 58–9.

It is, she adds in one of her wittiest asides, a distinction they share with the horseleech.[25] Now, of all Erasmus' gestures, none is more human or more beguiling than that he places himself in the Ship of Fools as one of the passengers. Folly is as universal in this world as lying was among the Cretans; the author of a tract on folly is no more exempt than Epimenides. So Stultitia makes fun of Erasmus' excuses and his knowledge of Greek, and later, when she is attacking the cult of saints, she will make an equivocal attack as well on the worship of a saint named Erasmus (ME 78). Similarly, in the *Cyclops* colloquy, Polyphemus argues that the world must be nearing its end because evil and corruption are so widespread: "people whore, buy, sell, pawn, engage in usury, build; kings make war, priests study to make money, theologians make syllogisms, monks run up and down the world, the populace is in tumult, Erasmus is writing colloquies: there is no end to the evils that beset us." [26] If Stultitia extends her irony to include Erasmus, however, she also extends it to include, finally, herself as well. She may excuse her use of Greek terms at this juncture by claiming that she does it to make fun of the bilinguists; but she continues to employ the device throughout the rest of her speech, in precisely the manner of those who, as she says, weave into their Latin orations some little Greek words as ornaments, even though there is no place for them.[27]

The next section of Stultitia's oration, in which she discusses her birth, education, and companions, can be located only with difficulty in the Quintilian schema. Hudson assigns it to the commencement of the confirmation, yet it seems more like an introduction to the confirmation than an integral part of it. Hence, in Leonard Dean's translation,[28] it comes as a conclusion to what Hudson would call the narration-partition section. The difficult arises from the fact that such a genealogy does not belong to an oration generally, but rather to an encomium specifically. In the paradigm for encomia established by T. C. Burgess on the basis of Menander, Aphthonius, Nicolaus Sophista,

[25] ME 7-8: "Visum est enim hac quoque parte nostri temporis rhetores imitari, qui plane Deos esse sese credunt, si hirudinum ritu bilingues appareant, ac praeclarum facinus esse ducunt, latinis orationibus subinde graeculas aliquot voculas, velut emblemata intertexere, etiamsi nunc non erat his locus."

[26] LB I.883D–883E: "Quoniam, inquiunt, idem nunc faciunt homines quod faciebant imminente diluvio, epulantur, potant, commessantur, ducunt, nubunt, scortantur, emunt, vendunt, foenerant et foenerantur, aedificant: Reges belligerantur, Sacerdotes student augendis censibus, Theologi nectunt syllogismos, Monachi per orbem cursitant, populus tumultuatur, Erasmus scribit colloquia: denique nihil malorum abest, fames, sitis, latrocinia, bellum, pestilentia, seditio, rerum bonarum inopia."

[27] See note 25.

[28] Leonard F. Dean, tr., *The Praise of Folly*, by *Desiderius Erasmus* (New York, 1949).

and others,[29] we find that the initial parts of an encomium are lumped together under the general heading *prooimion,* but that this is followed by a special section entitled *genos* or, by Anaximenes, *genealogia.* Under this genealogical section, there are generally four subsections: *ethnos,* the race whence the person praised has sprung; *patris,* his country; *progonoi,* his ancestors; and *pateres,* his parents. To these four may be added, if appropriate, a *genesis,* which refers to any special or unusual circumstances regarding the birth. Accordingly, Stultitia's discussion of her birth follows traditional precedent.

Her ethnos, progonoi, and pateres she describes negatively: "My father therfore was neyther Chaos, nor Orcus, nor Saturnus, nor any other of that olde and rustie race of Gods." Equally negative is the description of her genesis: she was not begotten out of her father's head, like Minerva, nor did he beget her in wedlock, but rather, as Homer says, "mingled in love." Therefore, the unusual thing about her birth is that it was not unusual. It was, indeed, so natural that, like Erasmus' own birth, it was not even legitimate. The father in whom she rejoices was Plutus, "the onely syre of Gods and men," author of *le monde renversé.* But lest the reader recall his Aristophanes, Stultitia quickly explains that her father was not the Aristophanic Plutus, worn-out and weak-eyed, but Plutus when he was young and vigorous, "full of hote bloudde, but muche fuller of *Nectar* drinke." This Plutus of whom Stultitia speaks with such filial devotion is the god of wealth—wealth that upsets the world and governs wars, marriages, and all human activities. But we must remember that this is also Plutus the god of plenty, companion to Demeter, who is responsible for the abundance of crops, good harvests, and the full breadbasket that Hesychius calls *euplouton.*

Stultitia's mother was Neotês, Youth, by far the fairest and gayest of the nymphs. Her patris, the mention of which provides one of those rhetorical occasions for the description of a *locus amoenus* which Curtius has traced through medieval literature,[30] was in the Fortunate Isles themselves,[31]

> where all thynges grow ["]unsowed and untilled["]. In whiche iles neither labour, nor age, nor any maner sickenesse reigneth, nor in the fields there dooe either Nettles, Thistles, Mallowes, Brambles, Cockle, or suche lyke bagage grow, but in steede thereof Gylofloures, Roses, Lilies,

---

[29] T. C. Burgess, "Epideictic Literature," *University of Chicago Studies in Classical Philology,* III (1902), 89–261; see esp. pp. 157–66.

[30] Curtius, *European Literature,* pp. 183–202.

[31] ME 11: "ubi ἄσπαρτα καὶ ἀνήροτα omna proveniunt. In quibus neque labor, neque senium, neque morbus est ullus, nec usquam in agris asphodelus, malva, squilla, lupinumve, aut faba, aut aliud hoc genus nugarum conspicitur. Sed passim oculis, simulque naribus adblandiuntur moly, panace, nepenthes, amaracus, ambrosia, lotus, rosa, viola, hyacinthus, Adonidis hortuli."

Basile, Violettes, and suche swete smellyng herbes, as whilom grew in
Adonis gardeins, dooe on all sides satisfie bothe the sente, and the sight.

These gardens that, as Shakespeare describes them, "one day bloom'd,
and fruitful were the next" and that served Milton as a kind of prototype for Eden were a land that almost every Renaissance poet was to
rediscover. The original source for these isles is, of course, the description of the land of the Cyclopes in the *Odyssey*, but one wonders if
Spenser may not have remembered Stultitia's own description of her
fatherland, where nature is triumphant and luxuriant and where "Ne
needs there Gardiner to set, or sow,/To plant or prune" (*F.Q.*, III.vi.
xxxiv).

The rogues' gallery of attendants and companions that Stultitia
introduces after her description of the Fortunate Isles comes closest
to the category in the epideictic paradigm termed *anatrophê*, that
section of an encomiastic speech which deals with the special circumstances of the subject's youth. One might expect to find an extensive
and hilarious treatment of this, on the order of that which we find,
for example, in *Pantagruel*; but Stultitia, always more interested in
the present than in the past and, indeed, still in that time of youth
which would properly form part of the anatrophê, merely gives a
list of her nurses (Drunkenness and Ignorance) and her companions
(Self-Love, Flattery, Forgetfulness, Laziness, Pleasure, Madness, Sensu-
ality, Intemperance, and Sound Sleep). If they sound more like a gang
of juvenile delinquents than fit playmates for a goddess, that of course
is intentional. Foolery and roguery go hand in hand, and it is only to
be expected that the greatest fool of all should travel in the company
of the deadly sins, now expanded from seven to eleven. Such "unre-
strained loose companions," as Henry IV once described a similar band
of rogues, call up stock antipathetic responses in our minds; and just
as we ridicule the Fool, so we censure the rogues that attend her. On
the other hand, we have already seen that Stultitia may not be as
foolish as we may have expected, and the second of her nurses, Ignorance, has already been confused with Wisdom. The careful reader may
therefore be properly skeptical of his response to this simple list of
vices. By the time Stultitia has finished her speech, they, like everything else, will have been demonstrated to be something other than
what they seem. It is too early in the speech for Stultitia to reveal the
true nature of her companions here, for we would not believe her; but
as they are swept along with her in the flood of rhetoric to come, they
imperceptibly suffer a sea-change. With the exception of Philautia,
they are hardly mentioned again; yet when Stultitia has descended
from the pulpit, when the applause has died down and we think back
to the companions she has had, we are suddenly aware that she has
spent her youth not among vices, but virtues.

With this catalogue of companions, Stultitia finishes her introduction and moves into the central part of her speech, which may be divided into three sections roughly corresponding to Burgess' Aphthonian categories of *praxeis, synkrisis,* and *epilogos.* The first, the praxeis, concerns the achievements and attributes of Stultitia, or what Dean has labeled "The Powers and Pleasures of Folly." The second, which is more implicitly than explicitly a synkrisis, is an account of "The Followers of Folly." And the end of the speech, the epilogos, is the celebrated description of the "Christian Fool." Thus, the following outline may be set up to demonstrate the adherence of the *Encomium* to the Aphthonian encomiastic scheme as well as to the Quintilian oratorical paradigm.

APHTHONIUS	ERASMUS	QUINTILIAN
	⎧ Folly's greeting	exordium
	⎪ Folly will praise herself	
prooimion	⎨ extemporaneously	narration
	⎪ Folly will not deliver	
	⎩ a partition	partition
genos	Folly's birth	⎫
anatrophê	Folly's companions	⎪
	The powers and pleasures	⎬ confirmation
praxeis	of Folly	⎪
synkrisis	The followers of Folly	⎭
	⎧ The Christian Fool	
epilogos	⎨ Folly will not deliver	
	⎩ a peroration	peroration

Although such a schematization is essentially of interest only to the specialist in epideictic literature, it does at least demonstrate the position that the *Moriae encomium* occupies in this particular tradition, a tradition that was most familiar to Erasmus as it manifested itself in Lucian. In emphasizing the Greek rather than the Latin prototype for Stultitia's speech, I have not wished to detract from Hudson's contribution to our understanding of the structure of this oration; what is important above all is to recognize, as he did, that Erasmus' work is classical in nature. But the Aphthonian paradigm, in exposing the component parts of what Quintilian calls the confirmation, does reveal the further important fact that it is the praxeis, not the synkrisis, that is the central section of Stultitia's speech. The praxeis, "The Powers and Pleasures of Folly," occupies not only the most predominant position, but something close to half of the length of the entire speech: in an edition of eighty-nine pages, the synkrisis takes up twenty-seven pages, whereas the praxeis takes up thirty-nine, or half again as many. This is highly significant for any understanding of the *Encomium.*

When the average reader has remembered this book, he has been most likely to remember the synkrisis, the attacks on the clergy, the princes, the papacy, and other estates. This is the section most discussed by commentators, just as it was the section most notorious, because most scandalous, in Erasmus' own day. But if Erasmus' little book has been largely misunderstood, one of the main reasons is that too much attention has been focused upon his description of Stultitia's followers and not enough on Stultitia herself and what she stands for. To be sure, the synkrisis is easier to understand than the praxeis: the synkrisis is constructed out of a simple satire that is mere invective, whereas the subtler ironies of the praxeis are those of the introductory parts of the *Encomium*, many-faceted and often self-contradictory. One senses that the attack on the monks and princes was written in a different spirit, as well as in a different style and with a cruder satire, and it may even be that this was the part Erasmus added, almost as an afterthought, after his friends in Chelsea had urged him to continue the work he read to them.[32]

In any event, if the pages to follow seem to slight the description of Stultitia's followers and to concentrate more upon the description of Stultitia herself, the reason is simply that the former is better known and more easily understood, whereas the latter is not only more elusive but contains the central and most original part of Erasmus' argument. The figure of the Fool dominates her speech; the nature of her folly lies at the heart of her message. The jesting equivalent of the serious philosophy expounded in the *Enchiridion militis christiani*—which is what Erasmus claimed the *Encomium* was[33]—is to be found not so much in the plangent laments and angry denunciations of the folly of the sixteenth-century world as in the lambent ironies and laughing praise with which Stultitia describes her own true nature.

[32] EE II.94: "Operis incoepti gustum amiculis aliquot exhibui, quo iucundior esset risus cum pluribus communis. Quibus cum vehementer placuisset, instituerunt vti pergerem. Obsecutus sum . . ."

[33] EE II.93: "Nec aliud omnino sectauimus in Moria quam quod in caeteris lucubrationibus, tametsi via diuersa. In Enchiridio simpliciter Christianae vitae formam tradidimus. In libello De principis institutione palam admonemus quibus rebus principem oporteat esse instructum. In Panegyrico sub laudis praetextu hoc ipsum tamen agimus oblique quod illic egimus aperta fronte. Nec aliud agitur in Moria sub specie lusus quam actum est in Enchiridio. Admonere voluimus, non mordere, prodesse, non laedere; consulere moribus hominum, non officere."

Problems of Paradoxes

by Rosalie L. Colie

One rhetorical paradox particularly rich in variations upon its own theme is Erasmus' *Encomion moriae,* obviously a praise of something conventionally regarded as unworthy of a proper oration. There is irony, if not also comedy, in the display of an author, by common consent the most learned man in Christendom, praising folly—but that oddity is but the beginning of an infinite chain of dependent anomalies.

First of all, what was being praised? We are never quite sure: the speaker, Folly, shifts her ground again and again. Sometimes folly seems a "good," as in the golden world into which Folly was born, a natural arcadia full of harmless pleasures, where children were the proper and properly careless inhabitants. Sometimes folly seems more than a little uncomfortable, as in the second childhood of rheumy old men, or in the self-deceptive world of mortal lovers young, old, and middle-aged. Sometimes folly is not harmless at all, as in the long harangues against the monks and the sharp critiques of secular and ecclesiastical hierarchy. Folly's first golden world, an utterly natural one, was topsy-turvy as utopias are topsy-turvy; but the idyll of the book's beginning soon shades into the darker hatchings of the Christian-Stoical "real" world Folly criticizes (and, ironically, criticizes by the standards set by the Christian Stoicism she criticizes).

Folly introduces herself in a mock-classical mode: she was born, not as her enemy Athena was, out of her author's brain; but "naturally" (like love), the child of Plutus and Penia, into the generous world of Epicurean nature. From an Epicurean position,[1] Folly inveighs against the Stoics (usually considered the defenders of nature and natural law), whom she interprets as rigorists, bridling by their unrealistic

---

"Problems of Paradoxes." From Paradoxia Epidemica: The Renaissance Tradition of Paradox *by Rosalie L. Colie (Princeton: Princeton University Press, 1966), pp. 15–23. Copyright © 1966 by Princeton University Press. Reprinted by permission of the publisher.*

[1] Erasmus, *The Praise of Folie,* trans. Sir Thomas Chaloner (London, 1549), Aiii-B. All references are to this edition. For a study of Sir Thomas More's Epicureanism which is very useful to understanding Erasmus' use of the tradition, see Edward L. Surtz, S.J., *The Praise of Pleasure* (Harvard University Press, 1957).

regulations the natural expansiveness and variety of human life, rich as it is in experimental error. During the shifting course of Folly's argument, the Stoical position comes in for considerable criticism, from a Skeptical as well as an Epicurean point of view. Folly herself, skilled in *epideixis* as she is, points to herself as a Sophist leveling her critical gaze at all rigorist positions, asserting her confidence in a life in which to err is not only human but also highly instructive. Folly takes the empirical position, that man is a mistake-maker (or, as she says in various ways, that he is foolish), who learns only from the mistakes he makes (or, that folly teaches wisdom).

Not for nothing had Erasmus elsewhere invoked Socrates, "O sancte Socrate, ora pro nobis." In his *Encomion*, much is made of the classic image for doubleness (and duplicity), Alcibiades' contradictory, paradoxical description of Socrates in the *Symposium*:

> For fyrst it is not unknowen, how all humaine thynges lyke the *Silenes or double images of Alcibiades,* have two faces muche unlyke and dissemblable, that what outwardly seemed death, yet lokyng within ye shulde fynde it lyfe: and on the other side what seemed life, to be death: what fayre, to be foule: what riche, beggerly: what cunnyng, rude: what stronge, feable: what noble, vile: what gladsome, sadde: what happie, unlucky: what friendly, unfriendly: what healthsome, noysome. Briefely the Silene ones beying undone and disclosed, ye shall fynde all thyngs tourned unto a new semblance.[2]   (Eiij)

Folly is as double, as duplicitous, as that Socratic box—and concerned to "disclose" from that box one of Socrates' major messages, "Know thyself." *The Praise of Folly* is a very peculiar exercise in self-knowledge, an exercise inevitably suspect by reason of its self-reference. For what do we know of Folly? Only what Folly herself tells us, Folly who all her life had been served by the merry companion Philautia, or self-love. As she tells us, Folly is accustomed to pointing her finger at things, things themselves, directly, empirically to indicate them as they really are. And yet that apparently objective gesture turns out to be subjective, since she, a member of a class, perhaps even that class itself, points directly at both other members of that class and at a definition for that class. Her discourse is all of folly: her encomium is a self-praise. She points her finger always at herself, as subject and object collapse into tautology, into infinite regression.

This self-reference "matches"[3] the epistemological operation, in-

---

[2] In his *Sileni Alcibiadis (Adagiorum Opus,* London, 1529, 753–63; separately printed, Paris, 1527), Erasmus lays out the philosophical contradictions reconciled in this figure. His witty exposition identifies the Silenus-figure with Antisthenes, Diogenes, Epictetus, various prophets and apostles, John the Baptist, and Christ Himself.

[3] For a continued discussion of "making" and "matching," see Gombrich, *Art*

deed; and like all reflection, this self-reference is mirrored again and again in the discourse. Folly confirms the form she has chosen, the paradoxical encomium, by appeal to ancient authority:

> . . . some of theym have not wanted, who with solemne styles, and much losse of slepe and candell, shewed at lest theyr folie, what ever theyr mattier was, in commendacion, some of this notable tryranne, some of that, some in praise of the fever quartane, others in settyng foorth what commoditees be in a flie, in baldnesse, or such lyke hatefull thyngs.   (Aij)

Paradox may give Folly license, but it does not escape her strictures. After a long critique of the quibbles of scholastic philosophers, Folly lumps the paradox itself in with those cobwebby time-wasters:

> I maie adde also hereto their *sentences or sawes,* which are so estraunge and beyonde all expectation, as the verie *Stoikes sentences* called *Paradoxes,* beyng compared to theyrs [the scholastics'], seme grosse, and more than vulgar.   (M)

The effect, of course, is to remove all standards by which the discourse may be measured, to keep the reference wholly internal, so that readers are constantly off balance, aware only of the infinite progression, or regression, implied in Folly's simplest observation on folly. Folly does not stop at mocking herself: she mocks her maker as well, first, by her references to the geographical locations particularly rich in fools, which of course turn out to be Erasmus' birthplace, Holland, and the part of the world where much of his youth was passed, Brabant (Biiij). In the list of saints idolatrously worshipped by the foolish and barbarous Christians of Europe, St. Erasmus appears—the saint of riches, therefore a patron particularly irrelevant both to Folly's moral system and to the scholarly life Erasmus himself led. Again, in the long list of fools' professions, the long comments upon rhetoricians, grammarians, editors, and Scriptural annotators point to the great fame of Erasmus as a member of all these groups. Once more, Folly does not simply dismiss these activities as worthless, for after having criticized the fatuity of Scriptural annotation, she praises, ambiguously, of course, the very "Annotacions" of Erasmus:

> But here (loe) me thynkes I heare how I am hissed at by some of these greke professours, who study scripture in that tounge, and make as though other doctours at these daies saw nothyng, nomore than crowes dooe whan their eies ar peckt out, whiles with certaine *Annotacions* of their owne, they goe about to duske mens eies as with smoke, amonges whiche sorte of notemakers, my friende *Erasmus,* whom

---

and Illusion, especially pp. 29, 73–74, 116–18, 186–89, 271, 356–58. See also Karl R. Popper, "Self-reference and Meaning in Ordinary Language," in *Conjectures and Refutations* (London: Routledge and Kegan Paul, 1965).

often for honours sake and good will I dooe mencion, maie be counted
the seconde, if not the fyrst.   (Qiiij)

Slightly less obvious, though very symmetrical, is the self-reflective
irony involved in the invocation by Erasmus, wisest of Christian
scholars, of Solomon, wisest of Old Testament sages—in order to
praise, not wisdom, but folly.

Folly's passage, so to speak, from Philautia to Solomon is significant
in indicating the trend of her curious discourse. Beginning within a
fully classical frame of reference, Folly's concern by the end of the
encomium has passed to an overwhelmingly Christian preoccupation.
Her sharpest strictures, throughout the discourse, were directed against
the hypocrisies and deceptions of self-styled Christians. In spite of her
skepticism of Scriptural interpretation, she herself cites and explicates
passage after passage from Ecclesiastes and Paul's Epistles (the second
a particular domain of Erasmus Roterodamus), in order to praise holy
foolishness and, therefore, herself. In her own presentation, the classical Epicurean figure changes into the Pauline fool of God: Socrates'
self-comment, that his only knowledge was that he knew nothing, becomes Folly's Christian comment upon her own nature. The Silenus-
box does turn inside out to reveal Saint Socrates praying for us. In
Erasmus' classical world there is a Christian sanctuary.

But even this observation, paradoxical though it is, is too direct a
statement for paradox to permit; Folly does not fail us in her final
self-contradiction and self-denial. Mocking her audience for its efforts
to follow her radically disrupted and distracting discourse, Folly takes
her equivocal farewell:

> But ones more forgettyng my selfe, *I passe my boundes* [in speaking
> of salvation]. Howbeit if ought shall seeme unto you to have been saied
> of me more knappisshely than became me, or with more words than
> neded, thynke I praie you, that I was the speaker, beyng bothe Folie,
> and a woman. Yet for all that remembre the Greeke proverbe, that *often-
> times a foole maie speake to purpose,* unless perchaunce ye thinke that
> this maketh no whitte for women.
> I perceive ye loke for an *Epiloge* or knotte of my tale, but than sure ye
> are verie fooles, if ye wene that I yet remembre what I have spoken,
> after suche a rablement of wordes powred foorth. The old proverbe
> saith, *I hate a tale bearer from the boorde*: But I saie, *I hate hym that
> remembreth what he hath sayd.* Fare ye well therfore, clappe your hands
> in token of gladnesse, live carelesse, and drink all out, ye the trustie
> servantes and solemne ministers of Folie.   (Tiij)

Her rejection of the value of memory extends to the value of all learning, dependent as it is on the collective memory of the race: she
undercuts and undermines her whole argument herself, to leave each
reader alone with the unpleasant realization that Folly has been con-

sistent to the last; "on all sydes like unto her selfe," she has abandoned
the reader to make his own decisions about value. True to Erasmus'
principles of free will, which he was ready to defend even against the
blunt pen of Martin Luther, Folly has left it up to each reader to
interpret her words as he can and as he must.[4] The fact that each man
will, in her view, make mistakes in that interpretation does not concern Folly: mistake-making serves man well, since his salvation depends
upon his ultimate realization of his own folly.

A formal aspect of the end of this encomium—and of many others
in the genre—is that it has no formal ending. The discourse stops,
certainly, but in such a way as to stimulate further thought in the
reader, even further speculation—Folly cuts off her own discourse, but
not discourse in general. Paradox, mocking formal limitation and
insisting on the continuity between thought and experience, formally
observes the decorum of its content. Erasmus, or Folly, has left his (or
her) discourse open-ended, stretching into infinity. One might risk
the further play, to suggest that paradox denies ends to assert the
importance of means.

Obviously, Folly (to say nothing of Erasmus) is engaged in *serio
ludere,* playing with the crucial problems of intellectual, moral, and
spiritual life, playing also with the men who take them too seriously,
as well as with the men who do not take them seriously enough. As in
the *Protagoras,* Folly's disquisition demonstrates that virtue cannot be
taught, even though knowledge and virtue are indissolubly one. John
Donne warned an anonymous friend [5] that paradoxes were naturally
generative—one paradox led to the making of another. Preoccupation
with Erasmus and the problems of Erasmian folly led a later Hol-
lander, Johan Huizinga, to propound his notion of man as characteristically *ludens,* a player of games of chance by rules made up by
himself.[6] Paradox, like Sir John Falstaff, is not only witty in itself but
the cause of wit in other men. Huizinga was witty in *Homo ludens,* an
extraordinarily illuminating book—and there is nearly as much incon-
gruity in Huizinga's brilliant but solemn exposition of his hypothesis
as there is in the thin and fastidious Erasmus' praise of eating, drink-
ing, and making love.

Another way of saying this is that the paradox, involving as it does
many different and varying figures of speech—prosopopeia and mock-
prosopopeia, irony, hyperbole—is nonetheless primarily a figure of

[4] In this connection, it is interesting to note how neatly the *Praise of Folly* fits
into the categories of ambiguity established by Ernst Kris (an art historian turned
psychoanalyst) and Abraham Kaplan: i.e., disjunctive, conjunctive, and integrative
ambiguity. Cf. their "Aesthetic Ambiguity," in Kris's *Psychoanalytic Explorations in
Art* (New York, 1952), pp. 243–64.

[5] Evelyn M. Simpson, *A Study of the Prose Works of John Donne* (Clarendon
Press, 1948), pp. 316–17.

[6] Johan Huizinga, *Homo ludens* (London, 1949).

thought, in which the various suitable figures of speech are inextricably impacted. Whatever else it is designed to do to incite its audience's wonder, the paradox dazzles by its mental gymnastics, by its manipulation, even prestidigitation, of ideas, true or false. The rhetorical paradox is, further, paradoxical in its double aim of dazzling—that is, of arresting thought altogether in the possessive experience of wonder—and of stimulating further questions, speculation, qualification, even contradiction on the part of that wondering audience.

The *Praise of Folly* can for a moment be reduced to the paradoxical *topos* of *docta ignorantia* originated by Socrates and developed so brilliantly by St. Paul and a host of Christian thinkers. The complicated and mystifying Socratic dialogue, the *Parmenides*, may be taken as the source of this *topos,* as of so much else in the paradoxical mode; since in the dialogue Socrates himself appears to be defeated by the logical acrobatics of Parmenides and Zeno. Technically, the *Parmenides* is a rhetorical paradox, since it presents two kinds of "unexpected" things. First of all, its material is full of surprises, as Parmenides and Zeno develop and reconcile their contradictory assertions; second, Socrates is, it appears, well and truly shown up by their dialectical subtlety. In the course of the dialogue's action, Zeno brings Socrates to acquiesce in notions quite contrary to those he asserts as his own, notions which, in an almost impenetrable irony, are also contrary to one another. The dialogue has remained a riddle to scholars,[7] and may perhaps be designed as such a riddle, in order to illustrate the pitfalls of purely metaphysical speculation. At its plainest, though, the *Parmenides* is clearly a demonstration of the axiom that paradox necessarily attends upon those men brave enough to travel to the limits of discourse.

[7] Francis Cornford, *Plato and Parmenides* (London, 1939), pp. 102–06.

Erasmus and the Tradition of Paradox

by Sister Mary Geraldine, C.S.J.

The paradoxical literature which became popular in England in the sixteenth century is usually thought to have been inspired by *The Praise of Folly,* which Erasmus wrote during his visit to More's home in 1509. Inspiration the *Praise* did, no doubt, provide, and pattern too in some measure, but the unique character of Erasmus's book needs some re-emphasis, for it differs in quality and, to some extent, in kind from the later essays which carry forward the paradox tradition in English literature, and indeed from the very works which the author lists as having provided classical sanction for such writing.

In spite of the haste with which Erasmus claims to have written his "silly little book," he took time to write a foreword and thereby to accession it. Let no one be astonished, he begs, at the triviality of his subject: let them but remember those eminent men who have previously written in such vein; and an imposing list follows—imposing but heterogeneous. Homer, he remembers, once sported with a battle of frogs and mice, Virgil with a gnat and a salad, Ovid with a nut; Polycrates, Isocrates, Favorinus, and even Seneca have falsely praised the unworthies of history; Lucian and Apuleius have eulogized the fly and the ass; certain other reputable ancients have praised baldness, fever, and even injustice.[1]

If Erasmus was himself casual in his classifying, it is not surprising that others, critics of his own time and later, were equally so. The *Praise* has been called learned parody, mock eulogy, an adoxographical essay;[2] and rightly so, for it is all that. But it is primarily satire, and

---

"Erasmus and the Tradition of Paradox" by Sister Mary Geraldine, C.S.J. From Studies in Philology, *LXI (1964), 41–44. Copyright 1964 by the University of North Carolina Press. Reprinted by permission of the publisher.*

[1] Erasmus, *The Praise of Folly,* trans. H. H. Hudson (Princeton, 1941), p. 2. All subsequent references are to this edition, and the title is shortened to "the *Praise*" where there can be no ambiguity.

[2] See, for instance, E. N. S. Thompson, *The Seventeenth-Century Essay* (University of Iowa Studies, III, 3), p. 95; Arthur Pease, "Things Without Honour," *Classical Philology,* XXI (1926), p. 41; Warner G. Rice, "The *Paradossi* of Ortensio Lando" (*University of Michigan Publications,* VIII, 1932), pp. 59–75; H. H. Hudson's introduction to the *Praise,* p. xx; Charles Lenient, *La Satire en France* (Paris, 1866), pp. 14–16.

the parody, eulogy, and paradox are geared to a serious moral purpose. It is no trifle, surely, to be shouldered easily into the group which Erasmus himself reviews, nor reduced to the level of its imitators.

Erasmus's list includes no work so complex as his own. Parody is not always panegyric, nor mock panegyric always parody; neither is necessarily satiric. Homer's *Battle* is parody but not mock praise; Virgil's gnat tale likewise; of the mock eulogies listed, only Lucian's two are parodies of rhetorical declamations; and of the fifteen works listed only five are satirical.

The *Praise* is unique in that it comprises all the qualities of all the works Erasmus lists. It is surely parody with the mocking Moria delivering such an oration as never before had followed the rules of rhetorical declamation. It is also an incisive and serious moral indictment of European society in all its aspects, an indictment that is sometimes eulogy, sometimes direct censure. It is, moreover, an oration that attempts, though awkwardly enough, to point in the end to that heavenly Jerusalem which sixteenth-century writers knew to be the end of any work of exhortation. Finally, and especially in comparison with contemporary works, it is a thoroughly human dramatic monologue, having as its satirical and allegorical device a woman. She is christened Moria because, like Europe, she is foolish, or perhaps because, like Thomas More, she is wise. Nonetheless she is no mere abstraction; she is a woman with a woman's varying moods, now confidential, now aloof, sometimes amused, often furious, ready to break her ironic vein to coax and plead, or to pursue some tangential thought; and she grows in folly or in wisdom as we listen to her diatribes and rhapsodies.

Although it is unlikely that Erasmus, who was not modest about his achievements, underestimated the worth of his work, it is surprising to find his Renaissance admirers failing to recognize its difference from other paradoxes. To some the *Praise* seems little more than a merry commendation of folly; others consider it a Jeremiad attacking immorality and ecclesiastical abuse. Sir John Harington, for instance, in *The Metamorphosis of Ajax*, mentions the *Praise* as one of many such pieces, serious treatments of light subjects, of which he cites seven. The *Praise* heads the list, although the other six are no more of its kind than is the *Metamorphosis* itself: "an encomium on the Pox, a defense of usury, a commendation of Nero," and so forth. John Grange, writing in 1577, does recognize that the *Praise* hides many profound reflections beneath a "cloke of mery conceyte," yet he couples Erasmus very easily with Skelton, whose good place in English letters is surely not in the Erasmian neighborhood. Not long afterwards Sir Philip Sidney points out that "Agrippa will be as merry in shewing the vanitie of Science as Erasmus was in commending of follie"; and although Sidney's final comment (that both had "another foundation than the superficiall part would promise") is sound, the casual juxtaposing of the mercurial Moria and Agrippa's sturdy denunciations is surprising.[3]

In all these paradoxes there is, of course, some common denominator by which we recognize them as cognate to one another; but an examination of the paradoxes and false praises current in sixteenth-century England [4] should, I think, justify the contention that Erasmus's *Praise* is not only superior to them, but (with one or two possible exceptions) quite different in scope and purpose. Its complexity is such that it seems to father two kinds of essay distinct from each other and germane only through this Erasmian progeniture. As mock eulogy and parody the *Praise* inspires some paradoxical essays delighting in clever urbane dialectic, little more than *jeux d'esprit;* as satire it is godmother to seriously didactic writing. Few of the works that follow in its train are similarly compounded of both toothless and biting wit.

[3] John Harington, *The Metamorphosis of Ajax* (1596), ed. Peter Warlock and Jack Lindsay (London, 1927), p. 8; John Grange, *The Golden Aphrodite* (New York, Scholars' Facsimiles and Reprints, 1939), sig. N$_{111}$; Philip Sidney, *An Apologie for Poetrie,* ed. E. S. Shuckburgh (Cambridge, 1891), p. 35. It is interesting to note that Thomas Nashe makes no mention of the *Praise* in his exhaustive lists of works similar to his "light friskin" of wit, *The Prayse of Red Herring,* although he opens the second of these lists with a sentence reminiscent of Erasmus. Nashe begins: "Homer of rats and frogs hath heroiqu't it." (*Works,* ed. R. B. McKerrow, III, 176); Erasmus's citation of other false praises and paradoxes begins: "Homer, all those ages ago, made sport with a battle of frogs and mice." (2).

[4] A survey which did not set itself limits of place and time would be too unwieldy for a paper of this size. Caspar Dornavius, in an anthology of some 1,130 large folio pages, *Amphitheatri Sapientiae Socraticae Ioco-seriae . . . Syllabus* (Hanover, 1619), has gathered together over a thousand items. Dornavius has been generous in his inclusions, canvassing from Homer to the writers of his own day, and including some verses and essays which surely have in them little of *sapientia* and nothing at all of the *ioco-seria.* Lines to a rose, for instance, or to a violet, are lyrical rather than paradoxical; Thomas More, or Henry Stephen, on the rustic life are true praises, not false ones. The items (all in Latin or Greek) are grouped according to subject matter, and no biographical or bibliographical documentation is supplied. I have chosen my "samplings" for this paper rather from the *Short Title Catalogue* (ed. Pollard and Redgrave) than from *Amphitheatrum,* but have made use of both.

The Praise of Folly and the Tradition of the Fool

by Enid Welsford

The Praise of Folly was written in 1509 during a visit of its author to Sir Thomas More and was published in France in 1511. Erasmus himself spoke slightingly of it, as being a mere trifle, but this was affectation, for he knew quite well that his indictment of society was no mere frivolity, but the fruit of many anxious meditations and pro- longed discussions between himself and his like-minded friends, More and Colet, concerning the prevalent social evils brought about by the depredations of unscrupulous money-loving princes and the alarming alliance between greed and superstition which was threatening the structure of the Catholic Church. If *The Praise of Folly* is comic, it is comic in the Meredithian sense: it is a most serious attempt to check the extravagancies of the anti-social by means of thoughtful laughter. But to understand Erasmus's method of procedure it is necessary to probe a little further than we have done so far into the contemporary conceptions of Folly.

The first thing to be remembered is that the words "fool" and "knave" were constantly coupled together, but not always in quite the same way; for sometimes they were treated as synonyms, sometimes em- phasis was laid on the distinction between them. To religious moralists such as Brant and Barclay, a knave was simply a fool regarded "sub specie eternitatis," for he was neglecting his true, ultimate self-interest, and what could be more ridiculous than that? In view of Hell and Heaven, the worldly man is penny wise and pound foolish as the saying goes. The writers of the sotties often adopted the same point of view and delighted to display the insignia of foolish knavery under various dignified, official uniforms. The fool was therefore the actually worthless character that lurked beneath the veneer of wealth, learning, and respectability. On the other hand the fool-societies were founded on the idea of the court-jester as the "sage-fool" who could see and speak the truth with impunity. From this point of view, the fool was

"The Praise of Folly *and the Tradition of the Fool*" (*Editor's title*). *From* The Fool *by Enid Welsford* (*London: Faber & Faber, Ltd., 1935; New York: Anchor Books, 1961*), *pp. 238–44. Copyright 1935 by Faber & Faber, Ltd. Reprinted by per- mission of Curtis Brown Ltd.*

the truth-teller whose real insight was thinly disguised as a form of insanity. There is a sottie, for instance, in which Mother Folly is entitled "La Reformeresse" [1] and is depicted as a severely moral critic of society. Whichever way up you turned the fool, he could be made an instrument for that reversal of convention which was the delight of the Enfants-sans-souci and other merry-companions of that type. Nothing could have been more congenial to the volatile mind of that great humanist than these variations of meaning, these ambiguities of definition, these possibilities of reversal and counter-reversal of accepted judgments, which enabled him to turn his *Praise of Folly* into a variegated picture of the life of his time and a masterpiece of subtle irony.

The dramatic vividness of Erasmus's imagination is illustrated at the start by Folly's opening words, which at once make us aware of the general stir of excited attention, the hearty clapping and laughter, the brightening faces which greet her arrival into the expectant assembly. It is a good beginning, and Folly takes advantage of her favourable reception to drive home her main point, which is, that although she may have no altars or temples, she is nevertheless the most universally worshipped and beloved and obeyed of all the deities who bear sway over human affairs. And, moreover, her popularity is justified, for she confers innumerable benefits, including life itself, upon the human race: "For since according to the definition of the Stoicks, Wisdom is nothing else than to be govern'd by reason; on the contrary Folly, to be given up to the will of our Passions; that the life of man might not be altogether disconsolate and hard to away with, of how much more Passion than Reason has Jupiter compos'd us?" For it is the passionate, unreasonable side of us that makes pleasure possible, that gives the enthusiasm and fervour which make people willing to take pains in pursuit of ideals of which even the graver sort approve; above all it makes men and women ready to enter into *Wedlock*, so that it is very ungrateful of the wiseacres of the world to depreciate the very Deity that brought them into existence. "For out of that little, odd, ridiculous May-game came the supercilious Philosophers, in whose room have succeeded a kind of people the world calls Monks, Cardinals, Priests, and the most holy Popes." And so half-seriously, half-mockingly, Erasmus defends the creative vital instincts of humanity against the encroachment of the analytic reason; and as a true humanist insinuates that the natural worldly life of married people is preferable to the life of celibates seeking a too-rarefied perfection. From this point of view folly is really the sane, normal life according to Nature. For after all

---

[1] Julleville, *Répertoire du Théâtre Comique en France au moyen-âge*. (Paris, 1886), p. 227; Le Roux de Lincy, A.J.V. and Michel, F., *Recueil de farces, moralités, et sermons joyeux, publié d'après les manuscrits de la Bibliothèque Royale par Leroux et Michel*. 4 vols. (Paris, 1837), T. I, no. 17; Picot, É., *Recueil Général des Sotties*. 3 vols. (Société des Anciens Textes Français), Vol. III.

man is the only animal who troubles his peace of mind by the inventions of tiresome arts and sciences; it was the insatiable curiosity of humanity which sullied "the purity of the golden age"; and even now "amongst these Sciences those only are in esteem that come nearest to common sense, that is to say Folly." But Folly is not only beneficial because she urges men to obey their vital creative instincts, she is beneficial because she fosters the pleasing illusions which make life possible. What would be our incentive to work, nay what our incentive to live, if we had no self-love? How could we enjoy love or friendship, how live in society at all, if we were not foolishly blind to the defects of others?

> Yet why this? will some one say. Have patience, and I'll shew ye what I drive at. If any one seeing a Player acting his Part on a Stage, should go about to strip him of his disguise, and shew him to the people in his true Native Form, would he not, think ye, not onely spoil the design of the Play, but deserve himself to be pelted off with stones as a Phantastical Fool, and one out of his wits? . . . And what is all this Life but a kind of Comedy, wherein men walk up and down in one another's Disguises, and Act their respective Parts, till the property-man brings 'em back to the Tyring House? And yet he often orders a different Dress, and makes him that came but just now off in the Robes of a King, put on the Raggs of a Beggar. Thus are all things represented by Counterfeit, and yet without this there were no living.

Here Folly strikes a sombre note, and seems to bid us join in the Danse Macabre and celebrate the essential vanity of human existence. But it is no mere cynicism; for as soon as we have been taught that "as nothing is more foolish than preposterous Wisdom, so nothing is more unadvised than a froward unreasonable Prudence," we are given the further lesson that the wisdom of the Stoics is not only inexpedient, it is morally unattractive. Seneca sets up as his ideal

> not so much as a Man, but rather a new kind of God, that was never yet, nor ever like to be. Nay, to speak plainer, he sets up a stony Semblance of a Man, void of all Sense and common feeling of Humanity. And much good to them with this Wise Man of theirs; let them enjoy him to themselves, love him without Competitors, and live with him in Plato's Commonwealth, the Countrey of Ideas, or Tantalus's Orchards. For who would not shun and startle at such a man, as at some unnatural accident or Spirit? A man dead to all sense of Nature and common affections, and no more mov'd with Love or Pity than if he were a Flint or Rock; whose censure nothing escapes; that commits no errors himself, but has a Lynx's eyes upon others; measures every thing by an exact Line, and forgives nothing; pleases himself with himself onely; . . . Nay, who had not rather have one of the middle sort of Fools, who, being a Fool himself, may the better know how to command or obey Fools; and who though he please his like, 'tis yet the greater number; one that is kind to his Wife, merry among his Friends, a Boon Companion, and easie to be liv'd with; and lastly one that thinks nothing of Humanity should be

a stranger to him? But I am weary of this Wise Man and therefore I'll proceed to some other advantages.

So far, although the wit of Erasmus is slippery as an eel, we are on the whole conscious of an undercurrent of approval as Folly lauds herself as wiser than the sage. But after a while there is a change of tone and even the goddess herself seems ashamed of some of her devotees, when she makes the usual roll-call of social types, and uncovers the absurdity of warlike Popes, worldly monks, crabbed scholars, predatory noblemen, rulers careless of the commonweal. Certainly at this point it is "La Reformeresse" who preaches, and her tongue becomes so sharp that she is obliged to pull up lest she should go too far and begin to speak out of character. "But it is not my business to sift too narrowly the lives of Prelates and Priests, for fear I seem to have intended rather a Satyr than an Oration, and be thought to tax good Princes while I praise the bad. And therefore, what I slightly taught before, has been to no other end, but that it might appear that there's no man can live pleasant unless he be initiated to my Rites, and have me propitious to him."

And so, executing a final *volte-face*, Folly abandons the direct onslaught on vice, and returns to her original and subtler method of the reversal of values. Once more Folly praises herself as the true Wisdom, but in so doing she lifts the argument on to a higher plane. For cannot she find support in the Bible itself for her self-praise?

> Nor can I give ye any reason why it should seem so strange, when Saint Paul imputes a kind of folly even to God himself. . . . Christ speaking to the Father sayes openly, "Thou knowest my foolishnesse." Nor is it without ground that fools are so acceptable to God. The reason perhaps may be this, that as Princes carry a suspicious eye upon those that are over-wise, and consequently hate 'em . . . and on the contrary are delighted in those blunter and unlaboured wits; in like manner Christ ever abhors and condemns those wise men, and such as put confidence in their own wisdome. And this Paul makes clearly out when he said . . . "It pleased God by foolishness to save the world," as well knowing it had been impossible to have reform'd it by wisdome. . . . And what does all this drive at, but that all mankind are fools—nay, even the very best?

But Folly goes further than this. Not only are the "foolish," the simple-minded, easier to save, the state of salvation is itself a kind of divine madness: in this world a wild recklessness about earthly goods, in the next world an ecstasy which renders the whole soul "beside herself" and swallowed up in love of the Divine. "But not to run too far in that which is infinite, to speak briefly, all Christian Religion seems to have a kind of allyance with folly, and in no respect to have any accord with wisdom."

These words of Erasmus suggest an important feature of fool-literature—its essentially "Christian" quality, of which *The Praise of Folly* is a case in point. Erasmus is usually regarded as a revolutionary humanist of dubious orthodoxy. Yet Erasmus might equally well be regarded as the last great representative of medievalism. He was a cosmopolitan scholar regarding Latin as the natural vehicle for his thoughts, his country was Europe, his learning was dedicated to the preservation of the Catholic Church, whose cause was to him the cause of civilization. "Erasmus," complained a Spanish writer twenty years after the publication of *The Praise of Folly*, "is destroying the whole church with his quips and jokes." Yet if Erasmus was acting as a jester he was acting as the jester of a Shakespearian tragedy, he was endeavouring to preserve the sanity of a mad and crumbling world. The fool was a figure who belonged to the fabric of medieval society, the popularity of the fool as a vehicle for comedy and satire was a symptom that ominous cracks were appearing in the building. Erasmus's later letters are full of references to himself as the impotent spectator of a tragic conflict which he knew must end in catastrophe.

Although the Feast of Fools originated in the Saturnalia and the Kalends, and was a recrudescence of paganism; although the macabre and satirical character of fool-literature was an expression of an age of transition; it was also profoundly in keeping with the spirit of medievalism or even of Christianity itself. Nothing could be more sharply contrasted than the fool of the sottie, and the aspiring tragic hero of Marlowe, or the self-satisfied courtier of Spenser. Nothing could be more incompatible than the respective tempers of Erasmus in his *Praise of Folly*, and Bacon in his *Advancement of Learning*. To the child of the Renaissance man was essentially great, and nothing except his own inertia need hinder steady progress in scientific knowledge and complete attainment of earthly happiness. To the medieval thinker, man was essentially vain, and it was only when he knew himself for the fool that he was, that he could become the lowly recipient of Divine Wisdom. Erasmus stood between two worlds and saw his vision of Folly. He was on the losing side. Now, in our turn, we begin to feel heretical misgivings as we listen to the "high astounding terms" of our scientific humanists, who for all their enlightenment cannot show us how to provide all workers with work to do, or comforts to enjoy, or an adequate motive for living peaceably together in a stable social order. "And thus the whirligig of time brings in his revenges."

PART TWO

View Points

Northrop Frye

The most elaborate form of low-norm satire is the encyclopaedic form favored by the Middle Ages, closely allied to preaching, and generally based on the encyclopaedic scheme of the seven deadly sins, a form which survived as late as Elizabethan times in Nashe's *Pierce Penilesse* and Lodge's *Wits Miserie*. Erasmus's *Praise of Folly* belongs to this tradition, in which the link with the corresponding comic phase, the view of an upside-down world dominated by humors and ruling passions, can be clearly seen. When adopted by a preacher, or even an intellectual, the low-norm device is part of an implied *a fortiori* argument: if people cannot reach even ordinary common sense, or church porch virtue, there is little point in comparing them with any higher standards.

*   *   *

The form used by these authors [*e.g.*, Erasmus, Lucian, Rabelais, Swift, Peacock] is the Menippean satire, also more rarely called the Varronian satire, allegedly invented by a Greek cynic named Menippus. His works are lost, but he had two great disciples, the Greek Lucian and the Roman Varro, and the tradition of Varro, who has not survived either except in fragments, was carried on by Petronius and Apuleius. The Menippean satire appears to have developed out of verse satire through the practice of adding prose interludes, but we know it only as a prose form, though one of its recurrent features (seen in Peacock) is the use of incidental verse.

The Menippean satire deals less with people as such than with mental attitudes. Pedants, bigots, cranks, parvenus, virtuosi, enthusiasts, rapacious and incompetent professional men of all kinds, are handled in terms of their occupational approach to life as distinct from their social behavior. The Menippean satire thus resembles the confession in its ability to handle abstract ideas and theories, and differs from the novel in its characterization, which is stylized rather than naturalistic, and presents people as mouthpieces of the ideas they represent. Here again no sharp boundary lines can or should be drawn, but if we compare a character in Jane Austen with a similar character in Peacock we can immediately feel the difference between the two forms. Squire Western belongs to the novel, but Thwackum

---

From Anatomy of Criticism *by Northrop Frye (Princeton: Princeton University Press, 1957), pp. 227, 309–310. Copyright © 1957 by Princeton University Press. Reprinted by permission of the publisher.*

and Square have Menippean blood in them. A constant theme in the tradition is the ridicule of the *philosophus gloriosus,* already discussed. The novelist sees evil and folly as social diseases, but the Menippean satirist sees them as diseases of the intellect, as a kind of maddened pedantry which the *philosophus gloriosus* at once symbolizes and defines.

Petronius, Apuleius, Rabelais, Swift, and Voltaire all use a loose-jointed narrative form often confused with the romance. It differs from the romance, however (though there is a strong admixture of romance in Rabelais), as it is not primarily concerned with the exploits of heroes, but relies on the free play of intellectual fancy and the kind of humorous observation that produces caricature. It differs also from the picaresque form, which has the novel's interest in the actual structure of society. At its most concentrated the Menippean satire presents us with a vision of the world in terms of a single intellectual pattern. The intellectual structure built up from the story makes for violent dislocations in the customary logic of narrative, though the appearance of carelessness that results reflects only the carelessness of the reader or his tendency to judge by a novel-centered conception of fiction.

The word "satire," in Roman and Renaissance times, meant either of two specific literary forms of that name, one (this one) prose and the other verse. Now it means a structural principle or attitude, what we have called a *mythos.* In the Menippean satires we have been discussing, the name of the form also applies to the attitude. As the name of an attitude, satire is, we have seen, a combination of fantasy and morality. But as the name of a form, the term satire, though confined to literature (for as a *mythos* it may appear in any art, a cartoon, for example), is more flexible, and can be either entirely fantastic or entirely moral. The Menippean adventure story may thus be pure fantasy, as it is in the literary fairy tale. The Alice books are perfect Menippean satires, and so is *The Water-Babies,* which has been influenced by Rabelais. The purely moral type is a serious vision of society as a single intellectual pattern, in other words a Utopia.

The short form of the Menippean satire is usually a dialogue or colloquy, in which the dramatic interest is in a conflict of ideas rather than of character. This is the favorite form of Erasmus, and is common in Voltaire.

Ray C. Petry

. . . Erasmus, as he says in all his *Apologies,* was bent on innocent funmaking; fun that was deadly serious, of course. It has been insisted

---

From "Christian Humanism and Reform in the Erasmian Critique of Tradition"

that here Erasmus wanted to shame people into rejecting folly for
wisdom. There is something to that, perhaps. Yet any such program
has always been a lost cause. Erasmus had much more at stake than
this. He sensed that foolishness and wisdom are inextricably linked in
the human protoplasm. Here again, the genius of his thought was a
rare blend of the classical and the biblical. It was a part of his regard
for the indefectibility of Jesus' maieutic and for Paul's commitment to
the divine foolishness of gospel preaching and teaching. The people
pilloried in the *Praise of Folly* are rendered wholly bare. Yet, what
comes to light is not merely the pitiful foibles of the human but, much
more, the redeemability by the Divine from the painfully ridiculous
and perverse. This is possible, when humanity throws itself on the
gracious mercies of God's omniscient dealing with men as they are.[1]

Erasmus was doubtless aware of the long history of "learned ignorance" and of ignorant learning.[2] He was sufficiently the graduate of
the *Devotio Moderna* and of the Greek "Agora" to yearn for humane
reclamation of the human by sophisticated collation and subtle col-
loquium.[3] But the *Praise of Folly* goes far beyond this literary conceit.
It takes up the baton from innumerable ancients, pre-Christians in the
ascendant; also from often unacknowledged, medieval practitioners of
the Christian tradition exercising the critical temper. Basically, as for
them, in the Erasmian prospectus, the divine foolishness of Jesus'
historic incarnation and of Paul's preaching was held to be a working
remedy for human pretentiousness and well-regulated, ecclesiastical
cant. It is no accident that in the *Enchiridion* and *Paraclesis,* in the
Greek-Latin texts and commentaries, in the numerous *Prefaces* and
Paraphrases, in the *Querela pacis* as in the *Dulce bellum inexpertis,*
and in the *Julius exclusus e coelis,* the most difficult people to save are
the sophisticated, and the powerful—most notably popes, princes,
kings, priests, monks and professors.[4] Reading the notes to the New

---

by Ray C. Petry, in Medieval and Renaissance Studies, *edited by O. B. Hardison,
Jr. (Chapel Hill: University of North Carolina Press, 1966), pp. 149–51. Copyright
1966 by the University of North Carolina Press. Reprinted by permission of the
publisher.*

[1] Cf. again the *Letter to Dorp* (Allen, *Ep.,* II, 103); Olin, *Erasmus,* pp. 64, 72–75;
and of course the *Moriae Encomium* in the entire last part. Cf. our note 8. In his
letter to Thomas More (Allen, I, 461, l. 50), Erasmus notes: "Ut enim nihil nugacius
quam seria nugatorie tractare, ita nihil festivius quam ita tractare nugas ut nihil
minus quam nugatus fuisse videaris. De me quidem aliorum erit iudicium; tametsi,
nisi plane me fallit φιλαυτία, Stulticiam laudauimus, sed non omnino stulte."

[2] See the literature on and texts from the Ps. Dionysius, Cusa, *et al.,* in Petry,
Mysticism.

[3] Note St. Axters, *La spiritualité des pays-bas* (Paris, 1948), p. 112, on the role of
the "rapiarium."

[4] Cf. *Dulce,* ed. Remy, p. 93, ll. 1090ff., p. 101, ll. 1185ff. This, and the apposite
caps. 39ff. in the *Querela pacis* (Bagdat ed., pp. 156ff.) show how far from the king-

Testament text and the *Paraphrases* makes perfectly clear how directly Erasmus had learned his gospel lesson. The proudest are the most lost, the most confessedly undone are the best candidates for heaven—be they played-out strumpets or monks in the grip of acedia. They, at least, may, like the fabled Magdalene, and Martin Luther, give up the battle waged on their own terms only to win the war that God has been fighting for them and in them all the while.[5] At this point Francis had written a biblical commentary with his life that confounded the entire hierarchy. As he hinted gently to Innocent III, the curia might be the last to know that the Gospel was back in business again.[6] Francis, Roger Bacon, Lull, and Cusa loved to talk about "idiots," each with his own gratulatory inflection. It cannot be argued that the *Poverello* was any less a fool by taking pride in being one. Bacon was all too self-satisfied in his analytics of balancing off human error with Greek-Latin "sophos." Cusa, for his part, knew so much about the inversions and perversions of folly and wisdom as to be slightly hamstrung at times. Yet none of these, or Lullian folly either, failed of the main insight. Lefèvre, who had his own version of divine wisdom and human folly, was no less humanizing and critically evangelical in his reforming than the others.[7]

Nevertheless, it was reserved for Erasmus to let out the accumulated pus of hierarchical pomposity and lay despair with a biblically incising blade. Hebrews 4:12 was truly at work in *Stultitiae laus*. The gospel itself was the apparently mordant critique that brought *sanitas* back

---

dom of pacific love the hierarchs often are. The *Moriae* is replete with examples of the peculiar jeopardy in which ecclesiastical leaders stand.

[5] Consult the *Paraphrases* on Matthew, cap. 23, LB VII, 119–24; and cap. 26, LB VII, 131ff. on the woman and the alabaster box.

[6] Bonaventura, *Vita*, 3:8–10; I Celano 13:32–33; II Celano 11:16–17. For an attempted reconstruction of the evangelical *Regula Primitiva Sancti Francisci* (1210), cf. J. R. H. Moorman, *The Sources for the Life of St. Francis of Assisi* (Manchester, 1940), pp. 51ff. Cf. R. C. Petry, *Francis of Assisi*, pp. 41ff., and the texts cited.

[7] Cf. the *Testamentum*, 4: "Et eramus ydiote et subditi omnibus" (H. Boehmer, *Analekten zur Geschichte des Franciscus von Assisi* [Tübingen, 1904], p. 37). For Bacon on human ignorance and the causes of error, see the *Compendium Studii*, cap. 3 (Brewer, p. 414), and cap. 5 *ibid.*, pp. 425–32. Further, on the difficulty of substituting true "sciencia" and "sapientia" for error, cf. Bacon's *Moralis philosophia* (Opus Majus VII) in the edition of De Lorme, pp. 136:11–157:5. Lull, like Francis, regularly exploited the "fool" motif. Cf. Petry, *Mysticism*, pp. 149ff., apropos of the *Blanquerna* and the *Lover and the Beloved*. Cusa was famed, not only for his *Learned Ignorance*, but for his *Idiota*. Cf. a convenient set of selections in M. de Gandillac, *Oeuvres Choisies* (Paris, 1942)—critical texts in the Heidelberg Academy *Opera*. A useful study of "Weisheit" and "Wissenschaft" in medieval spiritual context is found in F. M. Oediger, *Über die Bildung der Geistlichen im späten Mittelalter* (Leiden, 1953), the first three chapters, for example. Lefèvre (cf. Herminjard, I, 100, ll. 167f.), celebrated the divine wisdom available to the simple laity via the Scriptures. The religious orders had their own rules, but indispensable to simple Christians was their special "rule," i.e., the Word of Christ (*ibid.*, pp. 167–68).

to the exercise of the Christian tradition. And the operation was trans-
forming. It began with human vanity turned inside out and proceeded
with a stark mandate for all Christians to lay hold desperately on
God's reforming, truth-engendering therapeutic.[8]

Since, for Erasmus, the gospels and the epistles were primary, the
most rejuvenating hope for earthly pilgrims was to appropriate eternal
beatitude. The place to start was with the Beatitudes.[9] As a layman I
have long been amazed at the insouciance with which theologians,
preachers, and teachers of religion can accept these violent affronts to
reason and nature. Who, in his right mind, believes that the meek will
ever inherit the earth? Well, Erasmus held that Jesus was proclaiming
an open secret and that it boded good, not ill, for all who seized it in
faith believing. This was good news, even for popes and university
men, though especially for earth's dispossessed. There was hope for
everyone who dared to take Christ and his divine philosophy as a
realistic plan of action. The theme song of Erasmus' prefaces to the
New Testament was this: only by being inducted into the bible prom-
ises can the poor and heavy laden know that their burden is already
resting on Christ's heavily yoked shoulders.[10]

Naturally, the *Praise of Folly* is the setting for a gospel exposure of
a hierarchy given principally to ecclesiastical "busy work." They are
all too responsible for excessive rites, perverted sacerdotalism, and constant internecine strife. This is galvanized by princes of both worlds
and perennially abetted by power-mad clergy.[11]

The church in all her hierarchy is, ironically, at her redeemable and
redeeming best when reduced to human futility. It is this simple des-
peration that makes Christians out of pagans and theologians out of
plow hands.[12] It even renders priests and monks more than dead
weight on the Lord's battle wagons. This recognition of human folly
can lead to true repentance for all and to pastoral vicariousness for the
"servants of the servants of God." [13]

---

[8] Cf. the last part of the *Moriae*, and the *Paraphrase* on Matthew, cap. 14, LB
VII, 85.

[9] Cf. the Greek-Latin text of Matt. 5 in LB VI, 27–28; also the above note on LB
VII, 85.

[10] Cf. *Praefatio*, 3rd ed. to the New Testament text in LB VI: "Venite ad me omnes
qui laborates. . . . Nullum hominum genus à se repellit servator omnium, omnes
invitat ad refrigerium. . . . Non discernit virum à foemina, non puerum à sene,
non servum à libero, non privatum à Rege, non divitem à paupere, non Judaeum
ab Ethnico, non sacerdotem à laico, non Monachum à non Monacho."

[11] Cf. the whole tenor of the closing sections of the *Querela* and the *Dulce;* not
least the *Julius exclusus,* and the *Moriae,* LB IV, 481–86. Erasmus comes back to
this theme in a variety of *Colloquies* (see C. R. Thompson, index).

[12] *Paraclesis,* LB VI, 3–4: "Utinam hinc ad stivam aliquid decantet agricola. . . .
Ex his sint omnia Christianorum omnium colloquia."

[13] *Moriae,* LB IV, 491–97.

Eugene F. Rice, Jr.

. . . At the end of the *Praise of Folly* Erasmus calls this Christian wisdom a kind of madness, a divine folly which leads the soul away from
visible, corporeal things to the invisible and divine, until it is "wholly
rapt away in the contemplation of things unseen" and seeks and loves
only the supreme good which is God.[1] Such knowledge alone is white
as snow, pure and free of any blemish.

This wisdom is no rustic piety. It is a *sancta eruditio* rather than a
sancta rusticitas, a *scientia* whose source is not only Scripture but the
classics also. Erasmus warns his readers against those who oppose learning on the authority of Paul's *scientia inflat,* or say that immortality
was promised to the innocent not to the learned, and that if you know
Christ well you need know nothing else. It is ignorance, not learning
which causes pride; for, like Socrates, the more a man knows the more
he knows that he does not know.[2]

From "The Transformation of Wisdom from Knowledge to Virtue" in The Renaissance Idea of Wisdom *by Eugene F. Rice, Jr. (Cambridge, Mass.: Harvard University Press, 1958), pp. 158–59. Copyright, 1958, by the President and Fellows of
Harvard College. Reprinted by permission of the publisher.*

[1] *Praise of Folly,* trans. H. H. Hudson, 1941, p. 120ff.
[2] *Liber apologeticus Desiderii Herasmi Roterodami in quo refelluntur rationes
inepte barbarorum contra poesim et literaturam secularem pugnantium,* Albert
Hyma, *The Youth of Erasmus* (University of Michigan Press, 1930), Appendix B, 288.

Arthur E. DuBois

In the *Praise of Folly,* Erasmus strove to find a mean between pagan
hedonism and Christian-pagan Stoicism and between Stoic optimism
and Christian pessimism. His proper study was man. And inasmuch as
he leaned heavily upon classical (particularly those of Plato, Lucian,
and Seneca) and mediaeval notions of psychology, it was inevitable
that such an attempt should result in an ironic disquisition on folly.
One may be confident that the Christian called the Stoic a fool, the
Stoic called the hedonist a fool, and the hedonist called the Christian
a fool. But the matter went deeper than that. For in discussing the
human faculties, idealists like Plato, realists like Lucian, Christians
like Barclay, Stoics like Seneca agreed that there was an intimate connection between, on the one hand, madness and folly and ignorance
and crime and, on the other hand, passion and reasoning and sensing.

*From "Humanism and Folly" by Arthur E. DuBois, Sewanee Review, XL (1932),
448–50. Reprinted by permission of the* Sewanee Review.

Two great causes of crime were deemed to be madness and ignorance. Madness might be caused by disease, often explained by the doctrine of humours or passions. More often it was the result of giving way to an excess of passion, uncontrolled passion being the motivation of the madnesses of Hercules, Orestes, Ajax, Orlando, Tristan, and others; uncontrolled passion likewise calling forth worried observations upon madness from Swift, Johnson, and others. A person who was mad was a person out of his senses or out of his head or mind (reason). The passions therefore were considered to be the ultimate sources of madness, of mis-sensing or mis-reasoning, a chief cause of crime. And folly was a mild form of madness.

In addition to being a source of madness and therefore a cause of crime, with sensing passion was distrusted as being unreliable, worldly, and limited in scope. Things are not what they seem; the report of things made by the senses and the passions, the human faculties by which one establishes a direct contact or a relationship between one's self and the specific, is therefore misleading to body or soul. By their very natures, these faculties confine one to the world of externalities and furnish one with no knowledge of ultimate causes and effects, absolute relationships, universalities. Not only are they impotent in themselves to transport one beyond the immediate and the specific; they also distract the reason from paying its proper attention to the universal. Only the true philosopher will be free from the tyranny of the senses and the passions; in consequence, he will be deemed foolish, but only by the worldly wise, because he will often seem unaware of what is going on in the world about him. In short, to rely upon the senses or the passions exclusively is again to be foolish or mad. It is to be without reason.

In addition to madness, ignorance was considered a chief cause of crime. As Plato, Erasmus, and others agreed, there are at least two kinds of ignorance. The first is the ignorance of the child, of the aged, of the untutored. It is foolish as the child, the old man in second childhood, or the simple fellow is foolish. It is unreason, want of knowledge and of the self-control which it gives. It leaves a person open therefore to a tyranny of the passions, its effects being most clearly evident in the peevish vexations of the old man. It is to be combatted by culture and education, and significantly Plato warns friends of families not to pamper the passions of children while their fathers try to teach them self-control.

The second kind of ignorance is also foolish, and more vicious than the first because it is strengthened by knowledge or even by reason. Whereas the first is but want of knowledge or self-control which may even be humored on occasion and which is not self-sought, the second is wilful, a want of *right* knowledge. A person ignorant in this way is doubly vicious, for he is able to perceive what is good and yet to prefer something else to it and to justify his preferences by rationalizations: he therefore discountenances the true good *and* establishes a false good in its place. In contrast to him, who may be worldly-wise, the fool is utterly wise and becomes the prophet in classic folk-lorish tradition even as it is preserved by Yeats or Masefield. To this type of ignoramus belong pedants, politicians, patriots, fops, and others who make a passion of their reason until it becomes un-reason. They are mad too.

Antonio Iglesias

This letter, my dear teacher of humanism, is not written to the moralist who wrote the "Colloquies," nor to the sparkling and prolific letter writer, nor to the learned theologian and celebrated editor of the Greek New Testament and of some of the early Fathers of the Church, nor to the great controversialist of the Reformation. It is addressed to the humane and wise humanist and witty man of letters who wrote "The Praise of Folly." Your biographers tell me that you wrote this literary jewel in the autumn of 1509 while staying as an honored guest at St. Thomas More's cheerful mansion in Bucklersbury, and that you wrote it in *seven* days to detach your mind from the pains of lumbago and to play a learned joke on your beloved host by making its Greek title, "Moriae Encomium," mean both "The Praise of More" and "The Praise of Folly."

How shrewdly wise Folly acted in choosing you as her mouthpiece! Who else could have defended her more thoroughly, with finer eloquence, and with greater Christian charity? And, admirable Desiderius, in this short book charged and supercharged with irony, could you yourself say where the wisdom of Folly ends and the folly of your own wisdom begins? I, for one, cannot. What is clear to me is the all-infolding charity with which you and Folly judge all fools. For in this kindliest of satires there is neither bitterness nor hatred; none of Swift's savage indignation or of Voltaire's supreme contempt. What I find everywhere in it is an uncanny understanding and a profound commiseration for the countless follies of your fellowmen. Like a loving and indulgent father teasing his naughty children, you gently and wittily tease all and sundry: the babbling rhetoricians, playing both sides against the middle; the lawyers "weaving together six hundred laws in the same breath"; the proud of birth, the money-grubbers, and the adulators of the rich; the scientists claiming to know for certain what no man can find out; the theologians who are so happy in their self-

From *"An Open Letter to Erasmus"* by *Antonio Iglesias,* Saturday Review, *May 17, 1952, p. 24. Copyright 1952, The Saturday Review Associates, Inc. Reprinted by permission of the publisher.*

love rather than in their loving knowledge of God; your lazy and silly fellow monks blissfully happy in their ignorance and self-satisfaction; the kings and the ruling princes completely oblivious of their social obligations while they faithfully worship Folly together with their courtiers; and bishops, cardinals, and even popes slavishly aping these worthies instead of gloriously imitating Jesus Christ's life on earth. You spare no one, you except nobody, because no human being ever lives outside the boundaries of Folly's universal empire.

And yet you yourself managed with incredible mental agility to be her faithful mouthpiece and at the same time to escape from her sway to pass sound judgment upon what she is and what she does. For what really amazes me is the mysterious manner in which the rich complexity of your being is clearly manifested through the multicolored brightness of Folly's motley. How did you manage, Erasmus of Rotterdam, to reflect your inner being rightside up in this magic mirror that reflects so much that is human upside down? In this unmatched little squib of yours I discern, with astonishment and admiration, the universality of your humanistic and theological culture, the piercing penetration of your subtle intelligence, your lively and charming wit, your delicious sense of humor, your undeceived clear-sightedness, your razor-sharp critical acumen, your vast and profound knowledge and sympathetic understanding of human nature, your artistic refinement, the delicacy of your touch, the fastidiousness of your scholarship, your literary polish, the comprehensive irony that informs your jibes with their implied pleadings for tolerance and for a charitable understanding of man's shortcomings, and the spiritual loftiness of your Christian vision of the world.

It is precisely because you harmonized so successfully and so effectively in your life and in your work these remarkable talents, high accomplishments, excellent virtues, noble ideals, and lofty aspirations of yours—and also because our present need is so pressing and so great— that I have been emboldened to ask you to do us a very special favor: Will you come back to the earth once more for two or three weeks to write a "bigger and better" Praise of Folly for our edification and possible salvation?

Margaret Mann Phillips

The eighteenth century had its own reasons for appreciating the *Praise of Folly*: but it is a matter of speculation whether this apprecia-

From "Erasmus and Propaganda: A Study of the Translations of Erasmus in English and French" by Margaret Mann Phillips. First published in the Modern Language Review, *Vol. 37 (1942), 12–13. Reprinted by permission of the Modern Humanities Research Association and of the Editors.*

tion went deeper than the surface value. Actually, this book is one of the very few in which Erasmus allows himself to describe the irrational sides of human life. Folly, the speaker, is as Protean as Erasmus himself: she describes the effect she has on human affairs, and how she makes the wheels of the world go round, and at one moment she identifies herself with stupidity or weakness, with pride in little things, with pleasure that makes life liveable; at another she seems to be the force of Nature, without which there would be no love-making or begetting of children; at another she seems to express Erasmus himself as she praises humble simplicity in religious thought and laughs at quiddities and quoddities; and at the end of the book she has a passage on the ecstasy of the saints and the mystic life which makes it seem that she is identified with the super-rational activities of the soul. It is the recognition of mysticism that makes the book so strange in the hands of Erasmus; and if the reader, shocked, calls him to order by saying "But it's a crime to call mysticism folly," the answer comes pat. "But it's only Folly herself who says so." In fact, Erasmus makes his position entirely safe, and the fact that such an assertion is put into the mouth of Folly can be made to prove either of two possibilities: that mysticism existed for Erasmus and Folly is here his mouthpiece, or that mysticism to him was founded on rational thinking and it is Folly to call it super-rational.

However, enough of the book expresses his own views, as for instance in the satire of scholastic philosophy, to make it likely that Folly can be taken here too as his messenger; and if so, he is standing up on the one hand for common sense as against intellectual juggling, and on the other hand expressing a belief in the direct apprehension of Truth through faith. The eighteenth-century readers must have accepted the one and rejected the other. When Folly describes herself as the playful, robust force which gives zest to physical life, they probably applauded her more than Erasmus meant them to, but when she pointed out how much of the Christian religion was founded on lack of logic, how unreasonable it is to do good to one's enemies or give away all one's goods to the poor, and how far from common sense the religious enthusiast can be—here, where Folly is speaking in her own person and not in Erasmus's, the eighteenth century may well have taken him as a pioneer of anti-Christian as well as anti-clerical feeling.

Chronology of Important Dates

	Erasmus	*The Age*
c. 1466	Birth of Erasmus.	
1469		Ficino, *On Love*. Beginning of Lorenzo d'Medici's rule in Florence.
1474		Birth of Ariosto (d. 1533). Ficino, *Platonic Theology* and *On the Christian Religion*.
1475	In school at Deventer and Hertogenbosch (to 1484).	
1478		Caxton prints Chaucer's *Canterbury Tales*. Birth of Thomas More (d. 1535). Inquisition organized.
1483		Birth of Luther (d. 1546).
1484		Pico, *On the Dignity of Man*.
1485		Caxton prints Malory's *Morte d'Arthur*. Henry VII becomes England's first Tudor king.
1487	Monastic life as Augustinian at Steyn; secretary to Bishop of Cambray (to 1494).	
1488		Diaz rounds Cape of Good Hope.
1491		Savonarola's Sermon on the Tyrant.
1492		Columbus discovers America. Alexander VI elected Pope.
1493		Colet in Italy (to 1496).

1494		Dürer visits Venice. New Florentine constitution.
1497		Leonardo, "Last Supper."
1498		Savonarola burned. Machiavelli made second chancellor.
1499	First visit to England.	Skelton, *Bouge of Court*.
1500	*Adagia*.	*Everyman* written.
1503	*Enchiridion Militis Christiani*.	Death of Pope Alexander VI; election of Julius II.
1504		Michelangelo, "David."
1505	Second visit to England (to 1506).	Bramante commissioned to rebuild St. Peter's.
1508		Ariosto, *La Cassaria*. Skelton, "Philip Sparrow." Michelangelo, Sistine Chapel (to 1512).
1509	*Moriae Encomium*. Journey to Italy (to 1514).	Barclay, translation of Brandt's *Ship of Fools*. Ariosto, *I Suppositi*.
1511	*De Copia*.	
1512	*De Ratione Studii*.	Medici return to Florence.
1513		Leo X (Medici) elected Pope.
1514		Machiavelli, *The Prince*.
1515	*Institutio Principis Christiani*.	
1516	*Colloquiorum Formulae. Querela Pacis*.	More, *Utopia*. Ariosto, *Orlando Furioso*.
1517		Luther posts 95 theses.
1518	*Encomium Medicinae*.	Machiavelli, *Mandragola*.
1519		Death of Leonardo. Cortez begins conquest of Mexico.
1521	*De Contemptu Mundi Epistola*. Life at Basle (to 1529).	Machiavelli, *Art of War*. Melanchthon, *Institutiones Rhetoricae*. Luther excommunicated.
1524	*On Free Will*. Paraphrases of Gospels and Acts.	Luther, *On Free Will*. Peasants' War in Germany.
1525		Tyndale's translation of New Testament. Luther's marriage.

1526	*Christiani Matrimonii Institutio.*	
1527		Medici expelled from Florence. Death of Machiavelli.
1528		Dürer, *Treatise on Human Proportion.* Castiglione, *The Courtier.*
1531	*Apophthegmata.*	Elyot, *The Book Named the Governor.*
1532		Rabelais, *Pantagruel.*
1533		Birth of Montaigne (d. 1592).
1534		Rabelais, *Gargantua.* Act of Supremacy in England (King becomes head of Church). Jesuit order founded.
1535		Publication of Tyndale-Coverdale English Bible. Execution of Thomas More.
1536	Death of Erasmus. First English translation of *Colloquia.*	Calvin, *Christianae Religiones Institutio.*
1549	Chaloner's English translation of *The Praise of Folie.*	

Notes on the Editor and Contributors

KATHLEEN WILLIAMS is now Professor of English at the University of California, Riverside. She has written books on Swift and on Spenser.

ROBERT P. ADAMS, Professor of English at the University of Washington, was a fellow of the Folger Shakespeare Library in 1953 and 1956.

ROSALIE L. COLIE, Professor of English at the University of Iowa and Visiting Professor of English at Yale, was a Guggenheim Fellow during the year 1966–67.

LEONARD F. DEAN, formerly of the University of Connecticut, is Professor of English at New York University.

ARTHUR E. DuBOIS is Professor of English at Kent State University in Ohio.

NORTHROP FRYE is Professor of English at Victoria College, Toronto. This widely respected critic was a Guggenheim Fellow during the academic year 1950–51.

HOYT H. HUDSON (1893–1944) taught English, public speaking, rhetoric, and oratory at several American universities. He was Chairman of the English Department at Stanford University from 1933 to 1942.

JOHANN HUIZINGA (1872–1945), a famous Dutch historian, is best known for his *Waning of the Middle Ages* (1919). His biography of Erasmus was written for the "Great Hollanders" series edited by Edward W. Bok.

ANTONIO IGLESIAS (1903–53) is the author of *Culture's Emergent Pathway* (1948). His series of "Open Letters" for the Saturday Review dealt with Emerson, Milton, and Montaigne as well as Erasmus.

WALTER KAISER teaches English and Comparative Literature at Harvard.

SISTER MARY GERALDINE, C.S.J., is Associate Professor of English at St. Michael's College, University of Toronto.

RAY C. PETRY is Professor of Church History at the Divinity School of Duke University.

MARGARET MANN PHILLIPS of Cambridge is the author of *Erasmus and the Northern Renaissance,* a general study of Erasmus' contribution to European culture.

EUGENE F. RICE, JR., formerly of Cornell, is Professor of History at Columbia. He was a Guggenheim Fellow and the recipient of a Fulbright grant during academic year 1959–60.

PRESERVED SMITH (1880–1941), for many years Professor of History at Cornell, edited and translated Luther's correspondence and wrote *The Age of the Reformation*.

ENID WELSFORD, known for research in Teutonic and Old Prussian religion, has retired from the post of Lecturer in English at Cambridge.

Selected Bibliography

Allen, P. S. *Erasmus: Lectures and Wayfaring Sketches*. Oxford: Clarendon Press, 1934. Contains essays on various aspects of Erasmus' life and work.

————. "Erasmus' Services to Learning," *Proceedings of the British Academy*. Oxford University Press, 1925. Examines Erasmus' intentions in his life's work of translation and annotation.

Erasmi Rotterdami. *Encomium Moriae*. intro. Heinrich A. Schmid; trans. Helen H. Tanzer. 2 vols. Basle: Opperman, 1931. This facsimile of the 1515 Basle edition includes Holbein's illustrations, marginal drawings, and the notes of Myconius.

Erasmus. *In Praise of Folly*. ed. Horace Bridges. Chicago: P. Covici, 1925. This modern edition of White Kennet's 1683 translation is illustrated with Holbein's drawings as well as those of more modern artists.

Harvey, F. B. "Erasmus," *London Quarterly and Holborn Review* (July, 1936), pp. 303–20. One of the best biographical sketches of Erasmus.

Hudson, Hoyt H. "Current English Translations of *The Praise of Folly*," *Philological Quarterly*, XX (1941), 250–65. This and C. H. Miller's later essay (see below) discuss the merits of some of the various English translations of *The Praise of Folly*.

Huizinga, Johann. *Homo Ludens: A Study of the Play Element in Culture*. trans. R. F. C. Hull. London: Routledge & Kegan Paul, 1949. A fascinating study of the mingling of play and seriousness in culture. *The Praise of Folly* is one of Huizinga's examples.

Hyma, Albert. *The Youth of Erasmus*. Ann Arbor: University of Michigan Press, 1930.

Leyburn, Ellen Douglas. *Satiric Allegory: Mirror of Man*. New Haven: Yale University Press, 1956. Deals with several satiric allegories, for example those by Dryden and Swift, as well as with *The Praise of Folly*.

Malloch, A. E. "The Techniques and Functions of the Renaissance Paradox," *Studies in Philology*, LIII (1956), 191–203. Discusses the literature of paradox to which *The Praise of Folly* belongs.

Margolin, Jean-Claude. *Douze Années de Bibliographie Erasmienne: 1950–1961*. Paris: Librairie Philosophique J. Vrin, 1963. A valuable source of recent international Erasmus scholarship.

Miller, Clarence Harvey. "Current English Translations of *The Praise of Folly*: Some Corrections," *Philological Quarterly*, XLV (1966), 718–33.

————, ed. *The Praise of Folie by Sir Thomas Chaloner*. Oxford: Early English Text Society, 1965. A well-annotated modern edition of the first English translation of *Encomium Moriae*.

Miller, Henry K. "The Paradoxical Encomium with Special Reference to Its Vogue in England, 1600–1800," *Modern Philology*, LIII (1956), 145–78. Although this deals with a period later than that of Erasmus, it examines usefully the nature of the form Erasmus uses.

Rand, Edward Kennard. "Horace and the Spirit of Comedy," *Rice Institute Pamphlets*, XXIV (1937), 39–117. The last section of this three-part study deals with Erasmus' use of Horace's "legacy."

Saxl, F. "Holbein's Illustrations to *The Praise of Folly* by Erasmus," *The Burlington Magazine*, LXXX (1943), 274–79. A rather specialized, carefully illustrated analysis.

Schenk, Wilhelm. "Three Circles," *Dublin Review*, CCXXIV (1950), 66–81. A good general study of Erasmus' ideas.

Surtz, Edward, S.J. *The Praise of Pleasure: Philosophy, Education, and Communism in More's Utopia*. Cambridge, Mass.: Harvard University Press, 1957. This and the following make frequent brief references to Erasmus and his ideas.

————. *The Praise of Wisdom: A Commentary on the Religious and Moral Problems and Backgrounds of St. Thomas More's Utopia*. Chicago: Loyola University Press, 1957.

Swain, Barbara. *Fools and Folly During the Middle Ages and the Renaissance*. New York: Columbia University Press, 1932. Discusses very interestingly traditional attitudes to the fool, and relates *The Praise of Folly* to them.

Thompson, Craig R., trans. *Ten Colloquies of Erasmus*. Indianapolis, Ind.: Liberal Arts Press, 1957. Thompson's introduction contains a brief but excellent discussion of Erasmus as a writer.

Thomson, D. F. S., and H. C. Porter. *Erasmus and Cambridge*. Toronto: Oxford University Press, 1963. Erasmus' letters from Cambridge with an introduction on his friendships in England.

Thomson, J. A. K., "Erasmus in England," *Vorträge der Bibliothek Warburg* (1930–31), pp. 64–82. A discussion of the influence of Erasmus' irony and humor on English writers.

————. *Irony: An Historical Introduction*. London: B. Allen & Unwin, Ltd., 1926.

Trevor-Roper, H. R. "Desiderius Erasmus," *Men and Events*. New York: Harper & Row, Publishers, 1957. An excellent essay on the influence of Erasmus on European thought.

Zweig, Stefan. *Erasmus of Rotterdam*, trans. Eden and Cedar Paul. New York: The Viking Press, Inc., 1934. A readable biography and analysis of the major works.